Introducing Hosea
A Study Guide

Introducing Hosea
A Study Guide

W. H. Bellinger, Jr.

Smyth & Helwys Publishing, Inc.
Macon, Georgia

ISBN 1-880837-32-3

Interpreting Hosea.
A Study Guide

Printed in the United States of America.

The paper used in this publication exceeds the minimum requirements of American National Standard for Information Sciences-Permanence of Paper for Printed Library Materials, ANSI Z39.48–1984

Library of Congress Cataloging-in-Publication Data

Bellinger, W. H.
Introducing Hosea : a study guide / W. H. Bellinger.
viii + 120 pp. 5.5 x 8.5" (14 x 21.5 cm.)
Includes bibliographical references.
ISBN 1-880837-32-3
1. Bible. O.T. Hosea—Study and teaching. I. Title.
BS1565.5.B455 1993
224'.6'007—dc20 93-36590
CIP

Contents

For Jill and Chip

Preface

As I have written this study guide, two sets of events have permeated my thinking. One is the tragedy at the Branch Davidian compound called Mount Carmel near Waco. Those events raised in a vivid way questions of how we discern and hear voices that claim to speak for God—prophets. The other set of events is the suffering in what used to be Yugoslavia. The images of pain from those lands and from Mount Carmel have made me aware of how much pain is around us—in illnesses, in aging, in broken relationships, in the various dimensions of life. I hope our study of Hosea will help us think through how we hear prophetic voices and remind us afresh of the God who embraces pain.

The production of any manuscript owes much to many. I have avoided footnotes, but it will be clear that I am indebted to many scholars who have written on Hosea. I am grateful to Dr. Cecil P. Staton, Jr., and Smyth & Helwys for the opportunity to write this study guide. I am also grateful to Baylor University and my colleagues for a context in which to pursue my work. Walter Crouch, my graduate assistant, has provided invaluable help. The best editor I know is my wife Libby, and she has contributed greatly. The book is dedicated to my children, Jill and Chip, genuine gifts from God.

Using This Book

Two points are important in using the study guide. First, I have written it with the assumption that you will have the text of Hosea open as you read. You will need to follow

Hosea as you read my comments. Second, I have based my comments on the New Revised Standard Version (NRSV). The Hebrew text of Hosea is notoriously difficult, but for simplicity's sake, I have followed NRSV except where I found additional comment necessary.

W. H. Bellinger, Jr.

Introduction

Making a Start

The prophet is a person, not a microphone.
He is endowed with a mission, with the power
of a word not his own.

—Abraham Heschel
The Prophets

Imagine someone in your community coming forth to say that God has put you on trial and found you guilty of a life of falsehood. Or, this lonely voice says that the life of your community has caused God great pain and anguish! Imagine that this person claims that a marriage to a prostitute reveals a message from God and that the names of the children of that union announce God's intentions for you and your fellow citizens. Does that sound far-fetched? Perhaps so, but it is reminiscent of the prophet Hosea.

Most of you reading these words would first identify the name "Hosea" as an Old Testament prophet. This observation provides a good beginning point for studying the book of Hosea. Hosea is one of the prophets, and thus becoming better-informed readers of his book entails gaining some background knowledge on Old Testament prophecy.

Hosea was not the first prophet. There were other prophets in the ancient Near East and earlier prophets in ancient Israel. We read of Nathan, Elijah, Elishah, and

Micaiah in the pages of the Old Testament. Beginning with Amos in the eighth century BC, we encounter prophets who have books bearing their names, books we know as the Major and Minor Prophets.

Hosea's book is the first of the twelve Minor Prophets. These prophets are not minor in significance; they are only minor in the sense that their books, and usually ministries, are shorter than the Major Prophets Isaiah, Jeremiah, and Ezekiel. (Daniel is among the Writings in the Hebrew Bible.) In the Hebrew Bible, the Minor Prophets constitute a fourth prophetic book, one book called the Twelve; we could think of it as a book with twelve chapters. Hosea comes first in this collection, perhaps because his work was early in the era of the classical prophets. There is some evidence to suggest that later rabbis interpreted Hosea 1:2, "When the Lord first spoke," to indicate that Hosea should be at the head of the prophetic collection.

At the same time, Hosea might come first in the collection for theological reasons. Its tender and powerful beginning with the story of Hosea's marriage to Gomer as a sign of God's persistent love of the people certainly provides a significant beginning to the prophetic collection of the Twelve. In the second century BC, Ben Sira, a wisdom teacher, spoke of the Twelve as having comforted the people and given them hope and life (Sirach 49:10). Hosea certainly personifies that view of the Twelve, and perhaps that is why this book comes first.

We can make a start by seeing Hosea among the other prophets. Let us begin by describing prophecy and then consider its definition.

Old Testament Prophecy

The prophets spoke, first of all, as preachers. Their words were not initially tape recorded or distributed in written form. They were oral and spoken in public settings. Groups did not come to meeting rooms to hear the prophecies; the prophets went to the people. To get the attention of their audiences, these speakers often used vivid language. Hosea, as a preacher in ancient Israel, employed powerful and striking language in his oral communication with the people.

The prophecies are in poetic form. Poetry provides a powerful means of communication. Hebrew poetry is somewhat different from English poetry for which sound is so crucial. Although sound and rhythm are elements of Hebrew poetry, the thought conveyed by the poetry appears to be most central. Especially striking is the use of echo effects, parallel words and lines. Some verses in Hosea strike a memorable contrast:

> Ephraim has surrounded me with lies,
>   and the house of Israel with deceit;
> but Judah still walks with God,
>   and is faithful to the Holy One. (11:12)

Others betray similarity:

> So I will become like a lion to them,
> like a leopard I will lurk beside the way. (13:7)

The careful reader of Hosea's book will exercise sensitivity to such poetic form.

The prophets also spoke in short speeches called oracles, prophetic words from God. The book of Hosea is relatively brief, and it apparently contains elements of several prophetic speeches. Typically, prophetic oracles contain an announcement of God's coming action and a reason for that action:

> They shall eat, but not be satisfied. . .
> because they have forsaken the Lord. (4:10)

These oracles did not fall complete from heaven. They began in an encounter with God; in that encounter, the prophet was gripped by a divine message. Hosea 1:2 says that God spoke through Hosea; it is clear throughout the book that the message is from God. The prophet then reflected on this experience with God and worked at how best to proclaim God's message to the audience. Hosea effectively used a variety of images to that end.

Hosea also ministered and spoke prophetic words in a particular historical setting. He did not speak in Washington D.C. in the 1950s or in any other time and place except ancient Israel in the eighth century BC. The opening of his book makes explicit the historical setting, as do a variety of references in the book. We will return to the historical setting of Hosea's ministry because that information can help us experience the full impact of the prophecies.

After Hosea proclaimed poetic prophecies in his day, those oracles eventually came into written form and constituted what we now have as the book of Hosea. Remember that there were no reporters or stenographers or people with tape recorders following the prophet. Rather, the prophet and his followers remembered his words and began to collect them. These words may not have been popular at times, and so they had to be protected. Not long after Hosea's ministry, the prophet and his supporters began the collection that was eventually shaped into a book. When the northern kingdom of Israel fell in 722/1 BC, some supporters escaped to the southern kingdom of Judah and there preserved Hosea's prophecies. We do not know the identity of those who preserved and edited the book of Hosea or the other prophetic books, but they likely had strong ties to those who shaped the book of Deuteronomy with its emphasis on covenant.

It is important to remember that a prophetic book is not organized in the way a modern book is. It is organized more like a file drawer of prophecies in which one oracle reminds the collector of another. A prophetic book is a kind of prophetic sermon barrel. The prophecies are connected by themes and words rather than by some chronological plot or logical sequence common to twentieth-century western thought. Awareness that the book of Hosea came about by way of a process can help us read the book as a whole and seek to see its own organizing principles.

To summarize, prophecies were oral, poetic, short speeches in a historical setting and later put into written form. They proclaim a word from God to a people, and the prophet is important in this event of divine revelation. One of the conclusions I draw from this discussion is that prophhecies were meant to be heard and remembered. Perhaps we could thus become better readers of Hosea's words if we read them aloud in brief poetic sections and meditated on them before continuing.

The Nature of Prophecy

What was the prophetic task? The prophets certainly reminded their audiences of the history of their faith and looked to the future with God. They also spoke of the present from God's point of view. But their primary task was to announce what God was getting ready to do in the life of the community of faith and thus to urge that community to fullness of faith. Old Testament prophecy is not predictive in the sense of crystal-ball gazing into the distant future. Such an exercise falls to the gypsy at the carnival. Prophecy is about the future, though, announcing what God is about to do in the life of a faith community; in that sense it foretells. But it also forthtells, tells forth God's message, calling people to faith and faithfulness. As both foretelling and forthtelling, the prophets spoke of anticipated events of dread and events of hope.

The word "prophet" comes from a Greek word that means one who speaks, proclaims, on behalf of another. The Hebrew word is *navi'*, one who has been chosen to deliver a message. In international diplomacy, a messenger receives a message from one official and delivers it to another. A prophet receives a message from God and delivers it to the people. This message is tied to a particular setting; in what setting did Hosea deliver that message?

The Historical Setting

The first verse of chapter one functions as a heading or superscription to the book of Hosea. In the Hebrew Bible, it is the title of the book. It provides a historical framework for Hosea. At the death of Solomon in 922 BC, the united kingdom of Israel split into the northern kingdom of Israel with its capital at Samaria and the southern kingdom of Judah with its capital at Jerusalem where the Davidic kings ruled. The opening verse of Hosea names four kings from Judah—Uzziah, Jotham, Ahaz, Hezekiah—and one king from Israel—Jeroboam son of Joash, that is Jeroboam II. A listing of the kings from this period might be helpful:

Kings of Judah

Uzziah	786–742 BC
Jotham	742–735 BC
Ahaz	735–715 BC
Hezekiah	715–687 BC

Kings of Israel

Jeroboam II	786–746 BC
Zechariah	746–745 BC (6 months)
Shallum	745 BC (1 month)
Menahem	745–738 BC
Pekahiah	738–737 BC
Pekah	737–732 BC
Hoshea	732–722/1 BC

Israel and its capital Samaria fell to the Assyrians in 722/1.

Hosea prophesied in Israel not long after the work of Amos, beginning in the reign of Jeroboam II. 750 BC is a good estimate. The book's heading gives us the general era, the last years of the northern kingdom. The references to the succeeding kings of Judah indicate that Hosea's ministry continued into the last years of Israel. The first chapter suggests that the end of Jeroboam's reign is at hand. As you can tell from the list of Israelite kings, instability reigned in those last years in the north. Other international events from those years appear to be reflected in the book. There is, however, no mention of the end of the kingdom. Thus, a good date for Hosea would be 750–725 BC. Perhaps his work ended just before the fall of Samaria.

The reign of Jeroboam II is described in 2 Kings 14:23-29 as a time of expansion and renewed prosperity. The king's lengthy reign provided stability. At the same time, the prophecies of Amos show that all was not well in the kingdom. Social and economic distinctions were growing. Indications of economic plenty and political security were only apparent. Jeroboam's son succeeded him, but the reigns of the next kings were brief. When Menahem came to the throne in 745, he had brought an end to a dynasty and began his own line of royal succession.

The year 745 BC also brought another significant change, the resurgence of the kingdom of Assyria. Its history during this period is also important to Hosea. Egyptian and Mesopotamian powers sought to control the kingdoms of Israel and Judah. The geography of the biblical world accounts for that. Israel and Judah lived on the land bridge between Mesopotamia and Egypt, the two major centers of civilization in that part of the ancient world. Expansion of trade and economic prosperity was dependent on travel to such other population centers. Travel across the desert was not feasible, and maritime skills were minimal. The trade routes through Palestine were thus valuable. When the united kingdom of ancient Israel split after the death of

Solomon, the northern kingdom took most of the land and natural resources, but it was also more vulnerable to attack from the north. It was a prized possession. In 745 BC Tiglath-Pileser III, affectionately known as Tiggy, ascended to the throne in Assyria. He was an ambitious and skilled ruler and sought to expand his kingdom. Assyria became the bully of the region, and Israel initially submitted to their control under Menahem. But Israel also flirted with Egypt, and when Menahem's son Pekahiah became king, pro-Egyptian elements came to the fore. They resented Menahem's surrendering their independence to the Assyrians. The young king was assassinated and Pekah took the throne.

Pekah formed an anti-Assyrian coalition that received support from Egypt, but the main partners in the coalition were Syria and Israel. Thus began what we have come to call the Syro-Ephraimite War (735–734 BC). Syria and Israel, indicated by the name of its chief tribe Ephraim, sought by military action to force an understandably reluctant Judah to join their anti-Assyrian alliance. Shortly thereafter Tiggy came to punish the Israelite resistors. This move, in fact, marked the beginning of the end of the northern kingdom. Israel's throne was then seized by its last king, Hoshea. Initially, Hoshea submitted to Assyria, but he eventually began to flirt with Egyptian support. Shalmaneser V succeeded Tiggy and in due time invaded the disobedient kingdom of Israel and conquered it. It may well be that some of Hosea's latest oracles come from the time of Hoshea.

Thus, while Hosea began to prophesy in a time of apparent stability in the northern kingdom, his ministry continued into a time of considerable instability and uncertainty. These crises not only had political and economic dimensions, but they also had profound religious dimensions. Those dimensions dominated Hosea's proclamation.

The Significance of Hosea

The message of Hosea has retained significance. Most striking is the proclamation of Yahweh's love. ("Yahweh" is the special Hebrew name for God, mistakenly spelled as "Jehovah" in the King James Version of the Bible. Versions today often bring the proper noun into English as "LORD.") The prophet uses a variety of images to emphasize Yahweh's passionate love for the faith community ancient Israel. The story of Hosea's marriage also demonstrates God's love, even in the midst of divine judgment.

The other side of divine love is divine jealousy. That word may be problematic for some, but the Old Testament image is not one of a tyrannical, arbitrary husband suspicious of his wife's every move. A better translation of the word would be "zealousy"; when the Old Testament says God is **jealous,** read that God is **zealous**. God is zealous that the people of ancient Israel experience fullness in life, a fullness that comes only with faithful relationship with God. The judgment of God then derives from God's disappointed love. As God loves the people, they go away toward other gods. Dire are the consequences of their distrust of God; the consequences constitute divine judgment.

Another dimension of Hosea's message gives us the reason for the approaching divine judgment. The primary category the prophet uses to describe the people's disobedience is syncretism, the mixing of religions. The people still claim to be worshiping Yahweh their God, but they have been influenced by the fertility religions indemic to the land of Canaan. Those religions centered upon nature and fertility, and people had begun to think of their faith in Yahweh by way of the same models and theologies. The prophet attacks those tendencies with powerful rhetoric, speaking in terms of an adulterous relationship with God. Their adultery is idolatry. While not using the language of Baal, they have come to relate to Yahweh as a Baal, a fertility god. And the leaders of the northern kingdom of Israel have supported, indeed encouraged, that tendency. Such distrust of Yahweh will bring the people to naught, and the prophet rails against it and the leaders who support it. The coming divine action, judgment, will be the result of this disobedience.

Yahweh, the prophet urges, seeks not distrust and consequent death but a faithful relationship with the God who gives life. Such a relationship would issue in integrity and loyalty. The prophet announces Yahweh's intention to carry the people back to the beginning of their relationship to recover that original passionate love. But the path to that recovery of wholeness includes judgment upon their current infidelity. Hosea's proclamation is quite significant in the Old Testament view of a full relationship in covenant with Yahweh.

For most contemporary readers, the mention of the book of Hosea conjures up images of the marriage between Hosea and Gomer. That relationship leads us to read this book by way of the personal experiences of the prophet. Such a mindset makes it easy to forget that the story of Hosea and Gomer only takes up the first three chapters of Hosea, a book with fourteen chapters. Chapters 4-14 contain the prophet's poetic oracles. In fact, we do not know a lot about the man Hosea. The opening verse of the book gives us the historical setting of his work and the name of his father, Beeri. The following verses describe the tumultuous marriage of Hosea and Gomer and the birth of their three children. We can surmise from the book that Hosea was a native of the northern kingdom of Israel where he prophesied and that he was a man of genuine eloquence and insight. Beyond that, we know nothing of the person. This information about Hosea is important but hardly seems sufficient to provide a firm basis for interpreting the book.

Reading Hosea Today

I suggest we envision our reading of Hosea as a conversation between ourselves and the text. We come with life concerns and issues—and we need to be clear about identifying those—and enter into dialogue with the text. Some clarity about how that dialogue takes place might be helpful.

What do we do when we read a text like Hosea? Certainly we begin with a variety of expectations. We may expect the book to move in certain directions, and our expectations may change as we read. The beginning chapters on Hosea's marriage will certainly make a significant impact on us as readers and influence us as we move through the rest of the book. We then follow the rest of the book's sequence and how it relates to life. The text will lead us to join the prophet's audience in hearing the impact of these powerful words and focus on their significance. We will also become aware of the people in the book—Hosea, Gomer, the children, the people Israel, and God. What images of these characters does the book paint?

Indeed, what are the powerful poetic images Hosea uses to communicate?

Even though Hosea is an eloquent prophet, he does not tell us everything. Sometimes we must fill in the gaps, read between the lines, to get the whole story. One way to do this is to be sensitive to echoes of other biblical texts. This might help us to think about how we are putting together a full picture of what Hosea is preaching. The book will also refer to realities from its day. Getting some background information will help us. Finally, when we come to the end of the book of Hosea, we reflect on the meaning of the journey we have just taken through the book. How does it fit together, and what was its significance in Hosea's day? What is its significance today?

Attention to these dimensions of how we read Hosea can help us experience the power and relevance of the book. I hope this study guide will help with this process. I will provide questions to guide your reflection along the way and suggestions for further reading, but the primary task is to move through the book of Hosea, taking into account the various kinds of background information I have already alluded to, and consider its proclamation. We will do this in three sections: **The Marriage** (chapters 1-3), **The Law Suit** (chapters 4-7 and 8-11), and **The Call to Repentance** (chapters 12-14). My fervant hope is that this guide will help us all to hear God's message through the pages of this prophecy.

Questions for Reflection

1. In what historical setting did Hosea speak?
2. How did Hosea's prophecies come into written form?
3. How was the prophetic task similar to that of a messenger?
4. How are we to understand divine jealousy?
5. In what ways was Hosea's audience disobedient toward God?
6. How do the powerful images Hosea uses communicate to readers today?

Chapter 1

The Marriage

Hosea 1–3

". . . metaphor is pervasive in everyday life, not just in language but in thought and action."

—George Lakoff and Mark Johnson
Metaphors We Live By

Lakoff and Johnson have shown that metaphors, figures of speech in which qualities are transferred from one word or phrase to another through use of analogy, are not frivolous but are of the very essence of living; we live by metaphors. The biblical poets understood that. The book of Hosea uses metaphors to bring hearers/readers to consider the direction of their lives. Our entry into Hosea's prophecy is through the metaphor of marriage. It presses questions of relationship and commitment in life. After a look at the book's introductory verse, we will consider Hosea's marriage as a metaphor to live by.

Title (1:1)

The Hebrew text did not have "The Book of Hosea" as a title. Rather, the first verse served as the title. As is typical of Old Testament prophetic books, the verse speaks of the divine origin of the message, the prophetic messenger, and the historical setting. The opening phrase, "The word of the Lord that came," is characteristic of prophetic books (for example, Joel 1:1; Jonah 1:1; Micah 1:1; Zeph 1:1; Zech 1:1) and refers to a message to be delivered through a messenger. The Hebrew word translated "came" is from the verb "to be." A more powerful translation would be "The word of the Lord that happened to Hosea"; in the Old Testament, the divine word is dynamic and active.

This opening of the book's heading emphasizes the authority of the divine message in the book. The Old Testament prophetic word claims two bases of authority. The first is the divine call of the prophet, that is, the prophet is singled out, chosen to deliver Yahweh's message to the people. The opening phrase of Hosea 1:2, "When the Lord first spoke through Hosea," may reflect that call. The second basis of authority is access to the divine word. The Old Testament describes this access in terms of the prophet joining the council of the Lord, the gathering of Yahweh's messengers, in the throne room of God and receiving God's message for the people (Jer 23:16-22; 1 Kgs 22:1-40). Hosea had been called; his relationship with God grew as he had access to God's word. His message was of divine origin, and we are to read it as God's word.

The name "Hosea" means "salvation" or "deliverance," no doubt in reference to God's salvation. The name occurs elsewhere, and so our prophet is distinguished with a reference to his father Beeri, a name meaning "my well." All indications are that Hosea was a native of the northern kingdom of Israel and worked primarily in its capital Samaria.

Having referred to the divine origin of the message and the prophetic messenger, the introductory verse concludes with a reference to Hosea's historical setting. Hosea prophesied in the eighth century BC as did Amos, Isaiah, and Micah. I have already described the era. The fact that kings of Judah, the southern kingdom, are listed before Jeroboam II of Israel may be a clue that the book's audience included Judah. (See p. 5 above.) Hosea's message begins with an account of his domestic life.

A Wife and Children (1:2–9)

Prophets were from time to time instructed to act out their message. In this text, God tells Hosea to take a wife of whoredom and have children with her because "the land commits great whoredom by forsaking the Lord." The people have committed adultery in their relationship with God by going after other gods. That reality is reflected in Hosea's union with Gomer daughter of Diblaim, and Gomer and Hosea give birth to a son. As in Isaiah 7-8, God decrees the name of the child—*Jezreel*. Jezreel is a plain that separates Mount Carmel and Mount Gilboa in the Galilean hills. It was the scene of the bloodshed associated with the revolt of Jehu, a general who overthrew the dynasty of Omri around 842 BC. God will now avenge that bloody revolt at Jezreel. Jeroboam II (v. 1) was of the house of Jehu. He was succeeded by his son Zechariah, who ruled only six months before being assassinated. The house of Jehu came to an end. "The house of Israel" in v. 4 probably refers to the ruling house of Jehu rather than the entire kingdom. With the end of the house of Jehu, God has broken the "bow" (v. 5), the military strength of Israel. The bow was a feared weapon. The name of the first child then is a sign, associated with a place, that God will control the national life of the people. The name Jezreel means "God sows"; God is to plant the seed of the nation's political life, that is, determine its rulers. The judgment the name implies comes because the people have attempted to chart their national life without God.

In vv. 6-7 we hear of the conception and birth of the second child, a daughter, and of God's instruction to name her *Lo-ruhamah.* The name means "Not pitied"; God will no longer have pity or mercy on the house of Israel. The name of the child will be a living reminder that the sin of the people has outlived even the long-suffering forgiveness of God. The word used for mercy or pity here is the Hebrew word that refers to the womb. God's mercy is like the womb love of a mother, the love for the child to whom she has given birth. Ancient Israel has moved beyond God's motherly love and will no longer experience such forgiveness. But God does hold out hope for the kingdom of Judah, though their salvation will also not come by way of militarism but by the Lord their God.

When Gomer has weaned Lo-ruhamah, she conceives and bears another child, a son whose name is declared *Lo-ammi*—"Not my people." Since ancient times, Israel had understood itself to be God's people. That identity was based in the Creator's deliverance of the people from slavery in Egypt and confirmed in the covenant established on Mount Sinai through Moses. It was roundly understood to be permanent. With that background in mind, we can see how radical this prophecy was in Hosea's day. This child's name is a living sign that God is no longer on the side of the people. Their life as God's people is at an end. They have not been living daily as God's people but as people of the other gods; thus their status now will reflect their life—no longer as God's people. Their covenant relationship with God is at an end. That is a strong word, even for us. We have been so infused with the language of God's love, mercy, and grace that it is difficult for us to grasp fully the depth of God's judgment proclaimed so vividly in the names of these children. This early text in Hosea reminds us that there are painful consequences in life alienated from God.

Further Commentary (1:10–2:1)

Verse 10 of chapter 1 begins the second chapter of the book in the Hebrew Bible, and so it may be helpful to treat these verses separately. The reference here is probably to the united kingdom of ancient Israel since v. 11 speaks of the people of Judah and Israel. The verses focus still on the names of the children but in a very different way. The prophecy in the sign name of the third child, Lo-Ammi or "Not my people," is reversed to "Children of the living God." The language of the promise in v. 10 that the people will be like the sand of the sea recalls the promise of many descendents to Abraham and Sarah in Genesis 22:17. That great community will gather together under one leader and possess the land, a reversal of the prophecy in vv. 4-5 with the name Jezreel. The names Lo-ammi and Lo-ruhamah are reversed in 2:1. This passage seems to suggest an awareness of the full message of Hosea and may well be further commentary on God's word to the people. The full message of Hosea is of God's passionate care for the people. The reversal of the prophecies of judgment in the names here reflects an awareness of this passionate love. The import of the passage is that God's final word is not one of judgment but of renewal and hope. Indeed, the phrase "Children of the living God" (1:10) indicates an intimate parent/child relationship with God.

God and Israel (2:2–23)

The second chapter of the book serves to apply the marriage of Hosea and Gomer to the relationship between God and the people ancient Israel. It is an explicit and powerful proclamation against their involvement in Canaanite fertility worship. That worship reflected a nature religion tied to the cycles of nature and to the phenomena of nature. Its god was "Baal," in a variety of manifestations, which means master, lord, owner, husband. Baal was thought to grant fertility. The Canaanite view was that Baal died annually when nature died—such as in the frost of winter or drought of summer—and went to the underworld. There Baal found a mate and entered into a sexual relationship that brought fertility back to nature. Life is again possible. The religion was based in a cycle of sympathetic magic. Think of it this way: One goes to the sanctuary and participates in an act of fertility, imitating Baal, and the hope is that the act will induce the gods and goddesses to continue to do the same and shower fertility upon the worshipers. That was the purpose of sacred prostitution. This worship promised fruitfulness in all of life—family, agriculture, relationships, business, and other areas. I think we can readily see the temptation. With this kind of worship, the people would take care of their religious obligation and gain divine blessing, meet sexual desires, and enjoy worship. Canaanite fertility worship seduced ancient Israel, both literally and figuratively; their adultery against God was idolatry.

The general prophetic view is that such religion is death-giving. It gives only empty promises from a puff of hot air, a "not god," a nothing, a false lead, a god who is an empty idol. Hosea directly confronts that kind of religion in his day and boldly uses its imagery as a means of proclaiming a message that Yahweh is the only true giver of life, and thus the call to forsake Baal and return to the one true God.

The chapter begins and in a variety of places alludes to the first chapter with Gomer and the children. The alienation of wife and husband comes to the fore quickly as a symbol of the alienation between God and Israel. The prophet's plea is that the people turn from their "whoring," their running after the fertility gods, which has dire consequences (v. 3). Verses 2-5 are a graphic portrayal of Israel's going after other lovers, other gods, and the hope of finding fertility there: bread, water, wool, flax, oil, drink—all the things Baal promised. But God will hinder all this pursuit of other lovers and she (Israel) will not find them but return to the real giver of fertility, Yahweh. Yahweh was all along the one who gave the provisions of life—grain, wine, oil, and even the silver and gold used to make the idols of Baal. Verses 8-9 contain a strong dose of irony. God has given silver and gold, but the people use it for Baal. God has given grain and wine and wool and flax, but will now take them back in their season. The material was to clothe the nakedness of Gomer/Israel but her nakedness will now be uncovered and she will be shamed and all her greatly-valued lovers will be nowhere to deliver. The removal of clothing was a punishment for adultery and indicated refusal to provide clothing in the future. God may not be divorcing Israel, but the people have certainly given due cause for a barren future. They have broken their covenant relationship to God.

The worship of ancient Israel is corrupt ("mirth" in v. 11) and will come to an end. "Festivals" refers to the major festivals that require a pilgrimage to sanctuaries; local celebrations are referred to in new moons and sabbaths. All such appointed feasts will come to an end. The agricultural fertility that Baal was supposed to give will be destroyed and the land will become a jungle for wild animals. The mirthful Baal celebrations are sure evidence that the people have committed adultery in their relationship with God; they have gone after other lovers, gone whoring, forgetting and forsaking God. Worshipers no doubt still used the name of Yahweh, but the character of their worship and life reflected the religion of Baal.

The chapter has grown in intensity. It began with warning and moved to corrective measures and now to punishment. Verses 14-15 are pivotal; they offer renewal. God will "allure" Israel to the wilderness. The wilderness for Hosea alludes to the exodus experience, the first era of the people's history, the beginning of their relationship with God. Only the community and God were there, and the relationship was vital. It is comparable to the honeymoon period in a marriage. The reference to wilderness is precursed in v. 3. The wilderness period was certainly difficult but also foundational for the common life of the people. A move back to that time will serve to renew the relationship so the people can then move on again to Canaan and the additional era of their life in the land. In this renewed relationship, they can enjoy the fullness of life in the midst of the temptations of Canaan but remain faithful to the one true giver of life. Rather than sin, they can hope.

Verse 15 refers to the Valley of Achor ("Trouble") in Joshua 7. There Achan has sinned and is executed. The people are already disobedient and enter the land in dubious circumstances. Hosea now envisions a new entry to the land, one in which the relationship with God will be intact and offer a bright future, in which instead of Trouble will be a Door or Gateway of Hope. This word of hope would encourage Israelites who have remained faithful to God.

Verses 16-20 expand the implications of the renewed relationship between God and the people. This section is reminiscent of other prophetic passages that speak of significant future hope (Jer 31:31-34; Ezek 34:25-31) and have explicit messianic associations (Isaiah 11:1-9; 65:17-25). In the day of a restored and refreshed relationship with God, the people will use the address of "My husband" in their communication with God rather than "My Baal," a name that carries the connotation of ownership and mastery. That name, "Baal," will no longer be part of their worship. The prophet implies that even the name had been part of Israelite worship.

God will then "cut a covenant" with the people; that is the Hebrew idiom for making a covenant, formalizing a relationship. The cutting was probably of the animals used in the covenant-making ceremony such as in Genesis 15, but God will establish a relationship with the people that includes the destruction of militarism and war, especially of Israel's enemies so that the people will experience safety. In contrast to v. 12, the animals of creation and the people will live in full peace and harmony, and this relationship will be solidified for the future. God's relationship with the people will be characterized by divine righteousness, justice, steadfast love, and mercy. Righteousness refers to right relationship, in this case what God does to bring people into fidelity to that life-giving relationship. God's justice denotes equity in relating. "Steadfast love" or unchanging love is an important divine attribute in the Hebrew Bible. God's love or grace does not shift with circumstances; God is constant and loyal. We have already noted God's mercy as the womb love of a mother for her child. And finally, God is faithful, demonstrating trustworthiness in this relationship. God thus initiates this relationship, and the people shall know the Lord. The language of knowing is the same as that of the intimacy of a marriage relationship. It will not in any way be secondhand but intimate, personal knowledge by experience. The full and faithful covenant relationship between God and the people will continue intact.

The concluding verses of the chapter speak of fruitfulness in this future life. God responds to heaven and earth. This is an odd phrase, but presumably means that as a kind of natural chain, the creation has spoken a prayer for help on the part of the people and God will now respond through the earth by giving provision for life, grain, wine, and oil for Israel who is now represented as Jezreel. God will plant them in the land, a play on the meaning of the name of Hosea's first child, Jezreel, as "God sows." In a reversal of the names of negation, Lo-ruhamah, "Not pitied," will now receive pity, and Lo-ammi, "Not my people," will hear, "You are my people" and respond with "You are my God." This last reversal is a significant covenant phrase in the Old Testament. God initiates a life-giving relationship with the people by saying, "I am your God." They respond in faithfulness, "We will be your people." There are consequences as to how the people continue to respond, and the book of Hosea becomes part of God's message to instruct in proper response. The prophetic call is for the people to hear, to hearken unto God's communication that will bring completeness for the community.

One of the striking things about the second chapter of Hosea is the bold way the prophet uses the imagery of Canaanite fertility religion for proclaiming the message Yahweh has for the people. The people have been seduced, literally and figuratively, by the nature religions. Hosea contextualized his proclamation in a powerful, even risky, way. Jesus did a similar thing with Judaism of his day in the Sermon on the Mount with "You have heard it said of old, but I say to you." He used that phrase in Matthew 5:21-48 to place his instruction in a Jewish context but then to press it in radical directions. Paul also entered the context of his audience with his discussion of the unknown god on the Areopagus (Acts 17:16-34). It would be as if a contemporary witness went to an area of much prostitution and said to the prostitutes, "You have a real Lover. But unlike your 'customers,' this One genuinely loves you and will give you life in relationship and provide for you. But this Lover asks in response fidelity in the relationship." For most of us, that would be a pretty risky way to speak the good news.

Perhaps the prophet thus tells us something about God's intimate involvement with all of our world and our responsiblity to take the same stance.

The Return (3:1–5)

The concluding text of this first section of the book is brief but poignant. It moves us back more explicitly to Hosea's domestic life and so recalls chapter 1. The text speaks of God's intentions and attitudes toward the faith community ancient Israel in a way similar to the view espoused in Hosea 2:14-15. In chapter 3, Hosea speaks autobiographically of a divine command; the inclusion of the word "again" in v. 1 indicates that the account is of an additional event in the prophet's life. The command is to go and love a woman. The word "love" is used four times in this verse and strikes the theme and context for the chapter. The prophet is to love a woman who has a lover and is an adulteress. The description certainly calls to mind Gomer of the first chapter. This command is clearly put in the setting of a prophetic act that provided a powerful means of proclamation. These acts were object lessons for the prophet to act out God's message, but the ancients also believed that such power-laden acts really put into effect the fulfillment of the proclamation. Thus the prophetic act carried special significance in that day. Especially noticeable about the symbolic act dimension of this verse is the close parallel between the actions of the prophet and the actions of God. The prophet is to love a woman just as God loves Israel. The woman has a lover and is an adulteress; Israel has gone after other gods (lovers) as reflected in chapter 2 and loves raisin cakes. This last phrase is unusual, but it presumably is the case that raisin cakes, a favorite dish of the day, were an important part of the Baal worship the prophet condemns, and so the fact that the people love raisin cakes is parallel to their adultery, their unfaithfulness in relationship with Yahweh. Hosea is thus called to intervene in an unhealthy relationship and love this woman. God will do so also with Israel.

The second verse makes clear that it costs Hosea something to love this woman, just as it is costly for God to love Israel. God gives and initiates relationship (See Hos 2:19-20.) and suffers the pain of the people's incessant rejection. The material cost to Hosea for the woman is either a bride price or the cost of redeeming her from bondage. The cost, according to the Hebrew text, is fifteen shekels (silver coins) and a homer and a lethech of barley. A homer is a measure equal to ten ephahs and has been variously estimated at anywhere between fifteen and forty liters, perhaps somewhere between four and six bushels, or the load a donkey could carry. A lethech is apparently half a homer. The total value of one-and-a-half homers is another fifteen shekels. Thus the cost is thirty shekels of silver, the cost of a slave (Exod 21:32; Lev 27:4). The Leviticus reference is to the valuation of a free woman. This calculation of the cost does support the view that Hosea is buying this woman out of bondage, and that seems to me the most plausible view of the text, but as you can see, the calculation is not exact and it is probably unwise to pin too much on it. The point is that loving this woman is costly.

The prophet is pictured as doing what God has said, and immediately so. Hosea speaks to the woman and indicates that she must remain in a long period of confinement and discipline, but it is not a permanent circumstance. The woman is not to have sexual relationships, even with Hosea, during this extended time. The time of confinement will stop her unfaithfulness, the adultery that has been part of life up to this point.

The last two verses of the chapter apply this episode in the prophet's life to the relationship of God and the people; the verses give the meaning of the symbolic action. Hosea speaks of the sin of kings and princes. The princes were the king's officials: district governors, generals, and other leading members of the royal court. The people have sought to chart their national life without God, and in that sense these royal insiders have competed with God for the loyalty of the people. Such places of false confidence will not be allowed the people during their time of discipline. There will also be no sacrifice. Hosea here envisions the coming exile and destruction of sanctuaries. National and worship life will come to an end. Sacred pillars apparently represented idols or dead ancestors and were part of Canaanite religion. They penetrated Israel's worship at times and are rejected in Exodus 23:24 and 34:13 and Deuteronomy 16:22. The ephod and terraphim also refer to idolatry. An ephod could be part of a priestly garment but also referred to an image of a god or a means of predicting or divining the future (Jdgs 8:27; 17:5; 1 Sam 23:6; 30:7). Terraphim functioned in much the same way. They are known elsewhere in ancient Israelite tradition (Gen 31:19, 34-35; Ezek 21:21; Zech 10:2) and may have been the household gods, the spirits of dead ancestors who protected the house. They were shaped in some sort of human image (1 Sam 19:13-16), and their use is condemned in 1 Samuel 15:23 and 2 Kings 23:24. The people will be deprived in this disciplinary period of all those things which have led them away from God.

Following the period of discipline will come repentance. The hope of repentance has been anticipated in 2:7, 15. Now the people are able to move beyond judgment to hope. Note that the intervention of God in the form of disciplinary judgment initiates the return or repentance. The word "return" indicates that the people have been walking, living, one path and stop and turn around. They make a decision not to continue in the way of injustice and unrighteousness, and evil and faithlessness, the way that leads to death, but now to live based on what God has done for them. They choose to follow the way that leads to fullness of life, the way of justice, righteousness, faith, and relationship with God. They seek God, that is, they worship God. They will also give respect to the Davidic king, God's chosen representative to rule over the people of ancient Israel (2 Sam 7). The disciplinary time enables the people to come to God in awe. "Awe" is probably a better translation than "fear." The sense of the text is profound excitement, thanksgiving, exhilaration; that is, the people are thrilled to come to God. The picture is not a begrudged, forced return but one full of joy and expectation. The return is to the God who is gracious and gives good gifts, the God who is good. Such is Hosea's vision of the future to come. He envisions the disciplinary judgment that is to come and the hope for a genuine, life-changing return to God as a result. That hopeful view of joyful repentance beyond judgment resulting from God's initiative is characteristic of Hosea's proclamation.

The Marriage of Hosea

I have attempted to discuss Hosea 1-3 without too much attention to the details of Hosea's marriage. Let us now attend to those details. The marriage has long been discussed in treatments of Hosea, and it may surprise you to know that it has sparked a variety of controversial issues in the history of scholarship. Let me describe the issues, discuss some solutions, and bring our reading of these first three chapters to a conclusion.

1. The Historical Question. It may be surprising to many of us that the view that these chapters reflect a historical marriage between Hosea and Gomer has become important in the discussion only in relatively recent times. Many ancient interpreters understood the chapters in terms of visions or parables from the prophet about the relationship between God and Israel or God and the church. Some took a more literal approach, but the symbolic view dominated. For example, in the Targum—an interpretation of the Old Testament in Aramaic—the taking of Gomer and the birth of the children in chapter 1 is a symbol for preaching against sinful Israel, and chapter 3 is a divine speech to Hosea about God's love for this wayward people. Some recent scholars have taken the story as an allegory, but all the parts do not have symbolic value, such as Gomer's name, and the second chapter presses the story of the marriage in terms of the relationship between God and the people. That would seem less necessary if the story were an allegory. Others describe it as a parable. The story does have symbolic significance, as we have seen, but the text gives some details that imply a historical event: the names, the genders of the children, the weaning of Lo-ruhamah, and the price paid in chapter 3. The presence of these details has led most scholars today to view the marriage as a historical event.

I remember a student in one of my seminary classes who was always bothered by that view, and said, "But what would the neighbors say?" The student's question is, in fact, difficult to answer for a culture quite different from ours, but in a sense that is the point. The names of the children are especially for the purpose of getting attention. They are to be an ever-present, living memory of this proclamation, indeed a threatening memory. The story is unusual and so would proclaim powerfully. I take the story to be historical and as such to constitute a prophetic, symbolic act as an important part of Hosea's message.

2. *The relationship between chapters 1 and 3.* The reader of any English translation of this first part of Hosea will notice that chapter 1 is in the form of a third-person narrative. It talks about Hosea and the marriage and God and tells the story in this way: "The Lord said to Hosea. . . ." The third chapter is autobiographical, told in the first person: "The Lord said to me. . . ." That fact has raised a number of questions for interpreters. Also relevant is the second chapter, which is primarily in poetry and "applies" the story to God's relationship with the people. A number of interpreters have asked whether the first and third chapters might have come from different hands and have attempted to discern which might have been written first. Most, though certainly not all, commentators have suggested that chapters 1-3 came from a time early in Hosea's ministry. It would be difficult to make any kind of definitive statement as to which parts of chapters 1-3 might have come from different sources. What does seem likely is that chapters 1-3 of Hosea formed a kind of prophetic memoir from early in the prophet's ministry and that memoir became central in the formation of the Hosea tradition. Isaiah 6-8 functioned in a similar way in that prophet's tradition. The first chapter of Hosea begins the story and the second chapter interprets that narrative in terms of the relationship between God and the people. It especially plays on the children's names in chapter 1 and thus came after that first narrative. The third chapter also relates back to the first.

The description of the way chapters 1-3 fit together raises the question of how chapters 1 and 3 correspond to the events of the marriage. Which came first—the events of chapter 1 or the events of chapter 3? Or are the two chapters variant accounts of the same events? The decision hinges on the interpretation of the word "again" in 3:1. The word is taken in a variety of ways, but in any of them it tends to preclude the notion that chapters 1 and 3 are parallel accounts of the same events. Certainly for a contemporary reader of the Hosea story as we have it, the logical view is that chapter 1 came first and chapter 3 describes a sequel.

3. *The identity of the woman.* A related question has to do with the identity of the woman in chapter 1 (Gomer) and the identity of the woman in chapter 3. A number of recent interpreters have pointed out that chapter 3 does not name Gomer at any point and have indicated that it is unusual for the prophet simply to use the indefinite "a woman" in 3:1 if he is referring to Gomer. Perhaps, they suggest, we have read Gomer into chapter 3 for sentimental reasons. We find the story of Hosea's buying back Gomer to be a comforting image of God's costly forgiveness. It is certainly possible, with the indefinite reference, that the woman of chapter 3 is a different woman from Gomer (chapter 1). It seems unlikely to me, however, that a reader of the Hosea tradition would come to the beginning of chapter 3 in which the woman is described as having a lover and as an adulteress who is represenitive of an idolatrous (adulterous) ancient Israel and not immediately think of Gomer in chapter 1. Even the "Go **again**. . ." would bring to mind Gomer, the wife of harlotry. Thus it seems more likely to me that Gomer is the woman in view in both chapter 1 and chapter 3.

The other question about Gomer is the description of her as a woman of harlotry. That phrase has embarrassed a number of interpreters with our modern, middle-class, moral sensibilities. I suspect that that embarrassment may account for some of the attempts to see the story as parable or allegory. From our point of view, the command to marry a woman of harlotry and have children of harlotry is strange, but we must remember that Hosea lived in a very different context from our own. It is also important to remember that other prophets were on occasion commanded to do strange and difficult things. Isaiah wandered through Jerusalem naked; Jeremiah bought a field in enemy possession; Ezekiel, among other things, shed no tears at the death of his wife. The command to marry a woman of harlotry stands alongside other prophetic symbolic actions. Indeed, I believe we err when we put ourselves in the position of deciding if the divine command in the text is morally permissible; this would be a prime example of modern presumption.

We are still left with the issue of what the text means by a woman of harlotry. The most obvious interpretation for contemporary readers is that Gomer is a prostitute. Others have suggested that the phrase does not carry the connotation that prostitution would today; rather, Gomer is to be understood as one of the Baal prostitutes. We have already seen how sacred prostitution was a part of the fertility religion Hosea fought. A more recent view is that it was the custom of the day for women to submit to an act of sacred prostitution before marriage. The act dedicated the women to Baal and would thus symbolize the idolatry of the people. The evidence to support that view, however, is minimal; the view that such a custom was used in Hosea's day is quite speculative. It is possible that Gomer was a sacred prostitute, but I doubt we will ever establish that in any definitive way. Others have suggested that Gomer was not a prostitute when she married Hosea; the reference to harlotry in chapter 1 reflects the prophet's later realization that she had those inclinations all along. But chapter 1 gives no indication of such reflection; it simply associates Gomer with prostitution.

So what do we do with all these questions about the marriage between Hosea and Gomer? Our survey of the questions related to Hosea's marriage has shown that interpreters have taken a variety of views of the events described. One of the more interesting recent interpretations is that in G. I. Davies' recent commentary. (See the bibliography.) He suggests the following scenario:

> Hosea did not marry Gomer who was a prostitute; he became one of her clients, symbolizing thereby the apostate relationship of Israel to Baal. His three children are called **children of harlotry** because they were born of this extra-marital union. Later in his life, . . . Hosea "bought" and probably married another woman of immoral character, to symbolize Yahweh's love for his people Israel, despite their evil character. But he initially refrained from full sexual relations with her, to represent the period of discipline that would be required before Israel was ready again for an intimate relationship with Yahweh. (108)

Davies has convinced me that his view is possible; he has provided a fresh reading of these chapters. What Davies' work does make clear is that the text does not answer all our questions about the marriage; we are left to read between the lines. That cautions us not to pin our whole interpretation of Hosea on our view of the marriage in chapters 1–3. But the text does give us significant clues, and I believe it points to a more typical view of the marriage.

At the divine command, Hosea goes and marries Gomer, a prostitute. They have three children whose names carry symbolic significance. For whatever reason, whether inordinate guilt about her past or poor self-esteem or some other reason, Gomer leaves Hosea and goes after other lovers. Chapter 2 speaks of adultery. Again, in chapter 3, at divine command, Hosea goes and buys her out of the servitude she has fallen prey to and brings her back home to a period of discipline. The relationship of Hosea and Gomer is a prophetic act.

From the beginning of creation, humans have chosen not to trust God but have wandered from faithfulness. Even so, God chose the people Israel, wooed them and loved them and blessed them. Yet they kept turning away to idols, to Baal. There are consequences to their adultery, but God still loves them and will buy them back by way of disciplinary judgment. Such is Hosea's powerful prophecy to the people. This construction of the events and their significance seems to square best with the text and the message of Hosea.

The story of Hosea's marriage reminds me of two movies. The older of the two, "Cinderella Liberty," is about a sailor who falls in love with a prostitute and also takes in her rebellious child. When the couple tries to make a life together and have a baby, the woman is so confused that she runs away and seeks her former life. The movies ends with the sailor searching for her. His love continues unabated moving into the face of uncertainty. The more recent movie is the fairy tale "Pretty Woman." A wealthy business tycoon falls in love with a prostitute and seeks to have her make a life with him. She, however, seeks a whole life and relationship and will only join him in that circumstance. After initially declining, he seeks her out to go forward in hope. These two cinema narratives are but faint glimmers of Hosea, but they do remind us of the power of these first three chapters in the prophetic book. Faithful living may not be our greatest virtue, but we can find our strength in the unfailing and trustworthy love of God.

Conclusion

Our look at Hosea 1-3 has traversed a variety of issues. We began with the notion of metaphor, and there we end. In these chapters, marriage is the metaphor for life with God. Ancient Israel has committed adultery in that relationship; they have gone after idols. Still, God has not turned from them. God seeks a future for them, a future by way of a disciplining judgment. It would be a mistake for us to see only the story of the marriage of Hosea and Gomer in the book of Hosea or to sentimentalize the narrative. In addition, the gender relations in the story are not the point of its theology. It simply narrates a story from that cultural setting. It pictures a prophet and a God painfully and constantly seeking completeness in relationship.

When we read the book with this material at the beginning, marriage becomes the controlling image for Hosea's message. Will God's people be faithful to the marriage (covenant) relationship with God? Wholeness of life is found in faithful relationship with an unfailing God. Ancient Israel has gone whoring after Baal, but God's persistent and passionate care for the people will outlast even their adultery (idolatry). We ourselves still go astray, and we still hope in that same God, a God of redeeming and constant love.

Questions for Reflection

1. What does the name "Hosea" mean? How does that meaning relate to the prophets proclamation?
2. What does Hosea's marriage to Gomer signify?
3. How does Israel commit adultery against God?
4. How are the names of Hosea's children significant? Give the meaning of each name and its relevance to Hosea's message.
5. Describe Canaanite fertility religion and Israel's involvement in it.
6. What symbolic act does Hosea perform in chapter 3? How is this act significant?
7. What does Hosea 1–3 demonstrate about the character of God, for today's community of faith?

Chapter 2

The Law Suit (Part I)

Hosea 4–7

The prophet speaks not for himself but for the covenant. See 2 Corinthians 4:5 for an analogy: the prophet preaches not himself but the covenant; Paul preaches not himself but Christ.

—Walter Brueggemann
Tradition for Crisis

I have suggested that marriage is the governing metaphor for reading the book of Hosea as we have it. God seeks to give life to the "marriage" relationship. The question is whether ancient Israel will choose faithfulness, and that leads us to a second metaphor for the book, the law suit. The people are put on trial; have they been faithful? The people are then the defendants in this trial. God is judge and prosecuting attorney through the prophetic word. Various witnesses are called. In a sense, readers become the jury for they must judge the people's faithfulness and finally their own response.

The language of this section borrows from legal settings and suggests that Hosea's audience would have been familiar with a prophetic law suit. Micah and Isaiah also used the form. It seems unlikely that the text actually came from a trial in ancient Israel. Rather, the prophet, as often, is master of language familiar to his audience and uses such familiar images to proclaim the message God has declared for the people. The prophet continues to use the language of marriage so prominent in chapters 1-3 but here in the context of the trial of Israel's faithlessness.

A People Without Knowledge (4:1-3)

This brief section introduces the middle portion of the book and announces the theme. It brings the divine accusation both negatively and positively and then gives the sentence (v. 3). The chapter begins with a call for the people to hear and affirms, again, that the word is of divine origin and thus continues to carry import. The call comes because God has an indictment against the people. Given the legal connotations of the language, "indictment" is probably the best translation.

What is the nature of the indictment? It is first stated negatively in a pivotal line in Hosea:

> There is no faithfulness or loyalty,
> and no knowledge of God in the land. (4:1)

Faithfulness, loyalty, and knowledge of God are the prophet's key terms. Faithfulness has to do with truth and trustworthiness. The life of the people cannot be trusted; they are no longer true to God and have lost their way and have no integrity. In addition, the people demonstrate no loyalty, no unfailing love in relation to God or their brothers and sisters. This lack of loyalty in relationship means that the land has become an unkind place. There is also no knowledge of God in the land. We have already seen that this term does not mean knowing about God or an acquaintance with God. It rather refers to an intimate, experiential knowledge of God in relationship, a personal knowledge and commitment. This term is especially interesting for a variety of reasons, one being that it connotes the marriage relationship, the relationship gone awry among this people who knows not God.

If these terms indicate what is lacking, then what has filled the void in the land? Verse 2 gives the answer: swearing, lying, murder, stealing, adultery. The swearing entailed placing someone under a curse, a common custom of the day. A curse was considered a powerful weapon in battle, and conflict between people had become the order of the day. Also included are lying, perjury in relationship, killing, stealing, and adultery—again reminiscent of chapters 1-2. All of this carnage leads to a proliferation of murder, a particularly heinous crime for a society. (See Gen 4.) This list is quite reminiscent of the Ten Commandments (Exod 20), fundamental moral standards assumed in the relationship between God and the people. The people have habitually violated these standards and thus have lost their moorings. Ancient Israel could mount up lavish "worship" services, but that is not the true indication of commitment to God and community.

So we now have the charges, both negatively and positively. What are the consequences? The mourning of the land is a reference to drought from God; the land will dry up. As a result, people and animals alike suffer, languish. All of creation is in travail. Creation, and humans as part of it, is almost personified. All suffer as a result of the rot, the breaking of covenant, in that society. There is no knowledge of God and that leads to an unjust and corrupt community life. The result of that corporate corruption is trouble for the land and all—people, animals, or plants—in it. The drought, the thirst, is both judgment of God and result of sin.

Priestly Malpractice (4:4–19)

The rest of chapter 4 continues the theme of the opening section. At the core is the prophet's accusation of a corrupt priesthood that has led to corruption in the land. The rest of the chapter presses the accusation against the priests and the worship they lead and sees the consequences of corruption in the fall of the worship. It is not unusual for the text to move from a general judgment speech to one addressed to priests. The proclamation was likely made in a public place with priests present, perhaps in a sanctuary precinct. Priests are condemned in other Old Testament texts such as Amos 7:10-17, 1 Samuel 2:27-36, and Malachi 2:1-9. Here also the priests have forsaken their task.

The text of v. 4 is quite difficult, but it may be that the first two lines reflect the priest's attempt to silence Hosea. With the last line, the prophet responds that God is also bringing charges against the priest and continues to address that issue. Priest and prophet alike have failed in their task of leading the people toward knowledge of God. Deuteronomy 33:10 speaks of the task of the Levites as teaching God's law and instruction to the people as well as leadership in worship. That, no doubt, referred more broadly to the priests. They have not taught the knowledge of God to the people. The New Testament, in James 3:1 for example, also refers to weightier standards for those leading God's people.

The prophecy in Hosea 4 is a blistering one in the tradition of Amos 7. Prophet and priest will stumble by day and night; the image is of fumbling around in a dark room. Their families (mother and children) will feel the consequences of their negligence. Note the correspondence of guilt and punishment in v. 6: The priests rejected knowledge; God will reject knowledge of them as priests. They forgot God's law; God will forget their children. The reference to the prophet in v. 5 may be confusing to readers. Is Hosea pronouncing judgment upon his own colleagues?

Many of us grew up seeing prophet and priest in contrast to one another, but Old Testament scholars have come to see that the context in ancient Israel was rather more complicated. In a variety of Old Testament texts, prophet and priest are pictured alongside each other as part of the religious establishment in Jerusalem. The book of Jeremiah especially reflects this circumstance, and things were probably not very different in the northern kingdom in Hosea's time. In addition, there were a variety of kinds of prophets in that day; that is why the issue of prophetic authority is so significant, as mentioned at the beginning of this chapter. The prophet Hosea criticizes here is probably what we would call a false prophet, one proclaiming a gospel of prosperity that says not to worry about anything; God will take care of us no matter how we live. In that sense, the prophet is supporting the priest's religion of the day, a religion corrupted by Canaanite deities.

The reference to the priest continues in v. 7, though generalizing from what was probably a leading priestly family in vv. 4-6. This generalizing enables the prophet to move further toward a prophecy for the whole community. More priests and more priestly activity meant more sin.

The people may be in a glorious state of affairs now, but shame will come. Priests and people are then closely intertwined, "like people, like priest." The priests lead the people in the path of sin, and that path leads both of them to judgment. The failure of the priests to teach the knowledge of God has sealed destruction for the people. The last line of v. 10 makes clear that the sin is idolatry, ancient Israel's adultery. As a result, eating will not bring satisfaction, and intercourse—the reference is to some type of fertility ritual—will not bring children.

The image of the priesthood, indeed of the religious establishment of Hosea's time and place, is not very complimentary. They have led the people in a worship that partakes of popular elements of idolatry, and these religious leaders thrive off this state of affairs. The prophet again boldly borrows from the rhetoric of fertility religion to make the point: The community, leaders and followers, cherish harlotry; they have literally and figuratively gone whoring.

The description of this sad state of affairs continues and broadens to the general populace in the rest of this chapter. The people are drunk and without knowledge (v. 11) and worship idols. They worship and sacrifice on the high places, customary places of worship for Canaanite fertility religion. Verse 12 partakes of what Old Testament scholars have called the prophetic ridiculing of the idols. Isaiah 44:9-20, Jeremiah 10:3-5, and Habakkuk 2:18-19 illustrate the theme. How ludicrous! The people ask wood for direction, wood they otherwise use to make staffs for shepherding. With the latter part of v. 13, Hosea turns directly to the people and speaks of their adulterous lifestyle. Is the suggestion that their corrupt religion has led to the corruption of sexual values? Some recent commentators have suggested that the verse refers to a specific practice whereby brides participated in an act of sacred prostitution as a way of dedicating themselves to Baal before marriage. But we have already noted that evidence for the custom is minimal. Still, the verse indicates that both sacred prostitution and sexual promiscuity are rampant in society, but it is not the brides and daughters who bear the brunt of the proclamation. Rather the men, probably the leaders of the day, have set the tone with their sexual promiscuity and idolatrous worship. They use prostitutes and "worship" with "sacred" prostitutes. The term "prostitute" is probably a generic one; male and female sacred prostitutes were part of the ancient rituals. The picture the prophet paints of the community leads to the proverbial conclusion that a people without knowledge will come to ruin.

The concluding verses of the chapter continue the theme, and v. 15 expresses the hope that the southern kingdom of Judah will not follow the corrupt path of the northern kingdom. Gilgal and Beth-aven were famous shrines, places of worship in Israel and presumably where their idolatrous worship was enacted. Beth-aven means "House of Evil" and is a derogatory name for Bethel, "House of God," the well-known place of worship where Jeroboam I placed a golden calf. Gilgal and Bethel had been significant in the history of the people; now the cities are forbidden cities, symbols of the people's waywardness. Verse 15 echoes the language of Amos 5:5 and 8:14 in prohibiting worship, and oaths that were part of that worship at such places; it is death giving. But the people are now bound, "married" to idols and stubbornly so. They are drunk with the excitement of the adultery/idolatry, carried away with it like the wind. They will come to naught because of their corrupt worship, their shame, probably a reference to their idols, both gods and goddesses. Hosea uses Ephraim to refer to the whole people because it was the dominant tribe of the northern kingdom. The stubborn, unresponsive heifer, Israel, has taken a death-giving path. How can God feed them, provide for them, as the good shepherd does for the lamb? They remain unresponsive.

Chapter four describes a people without knowledge—without knowledge of God, loyalty or faithfulness. They flaunt their waywardness and reject all manner of instruction from God, especially the central Ten Commandments. What is more, their religious leaders lead, but in the way of idolatry. A people without knowledge is a people on the way to ruin; they self-destruct. They play with death-giving idols and become death. The themes of chapter four reverberate throughout the central portion of the book.

Faithless Leaders (5:1–7)

The themes of chapter 4 continue into this section. The prophet continues to rail against the faithless priests of the day as well as the rulers of the people. This section begins by addressing those who have led the people astray and continues with an account of the people's sin and its consequences. It is the faithless leaders who have really caused the downfall. This oracle was probably spoken in a setting with the leaders present, a large public setting, perhaps a festival.

The initial call is to hear and is addressed to the priests, the people ("O house of Israel"), and the king. All of them are threatened with the coming divine judgment. The word for judgment carries important connotations. It could mean "justice." The priests and kings were to maintain justice in the land, and now they will receive justice as judgment from God. Then, in characteristic fashion, the prophet identifies the corruption of the people with place names:

> for you have been a snare at Mizpah,
> and a net spread upon Tabor,
> and a pit dug deep in Shittim. . . .

Mizpah was important in the early history of ancient Israel's gatherings and worship as seen in Judges 20-21 and 1 Samuel 7;10. Tabor refers to Mount Tabor between the Sea of Galilee and Nazareth, referred to in Judges 4 and Deuteronomy 33. In the latter passage, it also is associated with worship. The first line of v. 2 is one of a number of places in Hosea where the Hebrew is difficult to decipher. If the reference is to Shittim, it probably refers to the place where the people camped east of the Jordan when coming out of the wilderness after the exodus from Egypt. Shittim is associated with the incident in which the people worshiped Baal-Peor, and that could well be Hosea's reference here. So we have three place names associated with worship. That is appropriate since the passage is addressed to priests, people, and king. The kings, along with the priests, in ancient Israel often were involved in the leadership of worship. Also notice that the prophet uses the imagery of hunting—snare, net, pit—for the leaders have trapped the people, caught them, and led them astray. There is real irony here for now the leaders will be caught in their own traps of false worship. God will now chastise all of them—priest, people, king, and their worship at Mizpah, Tabor, and Shittim. Chastising includes punishment, but punishment for instruction, as a parent correcting, chastising, a child. So the section begins with an address to the faithless leaders and moves to warning.

The proclamation continues with a full account of the corruption of the community and a straight-forward prophecy of coming destruction. The people cannot hide from Yahweh's presence and awareness of their life-style. They have gone whoring and are defiled. This language is quite characteristic of the prophet and refers to the adultery/idolatry of the people. The language speaks of the sin in terms of what is unclean and thus contagious. The contagion has spread among the people, and they are defiled. The prophet may actually be speaking of the corrupt worship practices in the land. Verse 4 speaks of the real dilemma in which the people find themselves. Is there no escape? The lack of knowledge with which chapter 4 begins keeps them from responding to the prophet's call for turning back to God. The people no longer realize that they have gone astray. The worship of the Canaanite idols, "the spirit of harlotry," has so engulfed them that they are not able to awaken from its power, and the community's life-style, "their deeds," controls life and fills their existence in such a way that they see no need to respond. Such a set of circumstances leads to Hosea's dire prophecies.

The emphasis on the people's lack of knowledge of their difficulties continues with the reference to their pride (v. 5). The prophet again uses legal language; part of the testimony against the people is their own attitude, their pride. It will lead to the fall, the stumbling, of the people. And Judah, the southern kingdom, will follow the same path. In the face of such dire warnings, the people will seek to worship God, "seek the Lord," with sacrifices, "flocks and herds," but they will not find God. God has now withdrawn from the people. What they find is absence, the absence of the God who is supposed to be present.

We ought not to read over this too quickly, for life in the ancient Near East was predicated on God's somehow being present in their worship. The absence of God meant great dismay. This prophecy is reminiscent of the prophecy of punishment in 2:7, that the people will go after their lovers (idols) and not find them. They shall now seek God and not find God. They have been faithless in their relationship with God. The people have broken their relationship, their covenant with God, and have had children of harlotry (2:4), those born with the help of Baal rather than God. These are alien children and so cannot inherit the land and its provisions which God gives.

I have read vv. 3-7 in terms of a prophecy of coming destruction; these verses could also be read in the present and refer to a set of circumstances already in force. The conclusion of v. 7 does seem to suggest a destruction that is coming within a month ("the new moon"); the people and fields will be devoured. I suspect that "the new moon" might well refer to a Baal festival that will lead to destruction; at least, a time of celebration will become a time of mourning. Faithless leaders have led the people astray down the road to destruction.

A Time of War (5:8–15)

Most scholars now agree that this section comes from the time of the Syro-Ephraimite War during the reign of Pekah (737–732 BC). By now, the bully of the region, the Assyrian Empire under Tiglath-Pileser III, has become a significant threat to Syria-Palestine. The northern kingdom of Israel

(Ephraim) and the kingdom of Syria (thus Syro-Ephraimite) have, in the face of that threat, crafted a mutual defense pact, a treaty that they will join in defending each other against the powerful common enemy. They want the southern kingdom of Judah to join their alliance, but the leaders there are skeptical. They believe resisting the Assyrians will bring destruction. In what seems to us a strange diplomatic maneuver, Syria and Israel seek to force Judah into the alliance by attacking them. If they controlled Judah, they could bring the southern kingdom into the alliance. Judah appealed to the Assyrians for help and received it, but the consequences for the region were severe. Hoshea took the throne of Israel and submitted to Assyria; thus began the end of the northern kingdom. 2 Kings 15:27-30 refers to the crisis, and Isaiah prophesied during this time in Judah. The crisis forms the backdrop of this section and so became the occasion for a warning cry from the prophet Hosea. As is true elsewhere, the northern kingdom is at the center of the prophet's concern, but Judah is also mentioned since that kingdom was also involved in the war.

Verse 8 clearly makes a new beginning with a cry of alarm and announcement of coming destruction in v. 9. The call is to arms, to blow the horn and trumpet. The horn was made from an animal's horn and used in worship settings but also in battle as a warning of approaching danger and as a means of gathering the troops. The trumpet, an instrument made of metal, and horn sound the alarm or announce the coming battle. The three cities mentioned here, Gibeah, Ramah, and Beth-aven (Bethel), were all in the southern part of Israel near the border with Judah and in the area of the tribe of Benjamin. The verse thus likely refers to an attack from Judah on the Ephraimite territory. This attack becomes the occasion for destruction that Hosea interprets as judgment from God. Israel finds itself in the midst of difficulty because it has strayed from God. A number of Hosea's prophecies indicate that the people have sought to craft their national life without an awareness of God's will and as a result judgment ensues.

Judah comes under scrutiny next. The first part of v. 10 indicates that they have made incursions into the territory of the northern kingdom.

> The princes of Judah have become
> like those who remove the landmark. . . .

A landmark was a stone that marked the boundary between owners' properties, and both Deuteronomy and Proverbs prohibit moving the landmark. It was an unwarranted seizure of another's property at which God becomes furious and pours out the cup of divine wrath. Because Judah has overstepped the bounds, Ephraim suffers, and the prophet recognizes this episode as judgment from God. The reason for the judgment is in line with the prophet's other pronouncements. In 4:6, Hosea characterized Israel as stubborn and here says Ephraim was determined to go after emptiness, worthlessness, vanity (v. 11). The Hebrew term used here is an obscure one, but could it also refer to the community's insistence on forsaking God and going after empty idols or empty ways of constructing a national life? This set of circumstances led to God's becoming a destroyer of Ephraim. Verse 12 uses two images; the first is that God is to Israel as a moth is to clothes; the moth is destructive. The second is of rot—God will bring rot to Judah. The two kingdoms are scheduled for judgment as they battle each other to preserve their corrupt, empty life-styles. Destruction grows like a cancer in their midst.

This war brought destruction to both kingdoms, and upon seeing that, the leaders of the two acted in ways characteristic of their common life. They paid tribute to the great king of Assyria, Tiglath-Pileser III, or they appealed to him for help. Ahaz king of Judah appealed to him for help in the war, and it may also be the case that Hoshea of Israel appealed to him for help after the war was decided when Judah sought to take territory from the northern kingdom. The nations trusted in this foreign alliance to the exclusion of God's help, but that route of political expediency brings no cure to the sickness and no healing to the wound. The people have failed to take God into account; God will now become like a lion. Political alliances will not change God's activity.

In this section, Hosea's prophecies carry a tone similar to those of Isaiah in the same crisis. The issue is not who keeps foreign allegiances but the heart of the national life of the people: Can they keep faith in God? God now speaks of acting like a lion, a lion hunting for prey, finding it and tearing it and carrying it off. No one is there to rescue the lamb Israel from the mighty divine lion. The lamb will be carried off to destruction. Hosea sees in the Syro-Ephraimite crisis a symptom of the empty life of ancient Israel. The prosecutor is gathering evidence, and the judge will pronounce the people guilty. The last verse of chapter 5 speaks of God's withdrawal as the prophet intoned in v. 6. The place to which God returns is not altogether clear, perhaps heaven or perhaps the wilderness if we take a clue from 2:14-15, but the point is that God withdraws. The verse carries a glimmer of hope, though, for it sees an end to the divine absence—when the community will, through the judgment that is at hand, realize that they need God and turn to true worship. Just as foreign diplomats seek the face of a ruler and then submit to the ruler, so the people will submit to God in worship. The people earnestly will seek to meet God.

Hosea suggests that faithless leaders have led Israel down the road toward destruction; that destruction is glimpsed in the Syro-Ephraimite War. The prophet continues to press God's case against the people and seeks to shake his audience into seeing that their expedient and simple solutions are not up to the task. They must delve to the heart of the matter, the matter of genuine faith in the one true God and faithfulness to their covenant relationship with God.

A Call to Hope (6:1-3)

These verses have occasioned a great deal of discussion among scholars. Perhaps the first question is whether to consider the verses as a continuation of chapter 5 or as the prelude to the remainder of chapter 6. NRSV clearly puts the verses with v. 15 of chapter 5 by using a colon as a connective. Hosea 6:1-3 then becomes the words used in the seeking of God described in 5:15, but there is no indication of the continuation in the Hebrew text. It has been added in early translations, into Greek for example, to make the connection. The first three verses of chapter 6 can stand on their own. At the same time, the verses do show some continuity of theme with the latter part of chapter 5 when they speak of the people being torn and stricken by God. Perhaps the best view is that these verses represent a reflection on the last part of chapter 5; that reflection brings forth the prophet's call for repentance after the difficulties of the Syro-Ephraimite War. It does appear that the distress prophesied in chapter 5 has come to pass by the time the first verses of chapter 6 are spoken. Hosea 6:4 appears to make a new beginning with its rhetorical questions, but we must come to the question of how the rest of chapter 6 relates to its first three verses later. The connection I have suggested between these first three verses and chapter 5 immediately raises the question of how to interpret the verses. A variety of options have been proposed, and they might be summarized as follows:

1. The verses contain words Hosea expects the people to use (or prescribes for their use) or words that the people actually use as a genuine expression of repentance.
2. The verses contain words Hosea expects the people to use or words that the people actually use as a false or inadequate expression of repentance.
3. The verses contain words in which Hosea urges his contemporaries to join him in returning to God.

The view that these verses are a false expression of repentance derives primarily from an attempt to connect the verses with vv. 4ff. of chapter 6, in which God speaks of the people's love as unreliable. But I have suggested that the primary connection is with chapter 5 and that 6:4 makes something of a new beginning. Some have suggested that the verses reflect Canaanite religion in being sure that God will save, in promising showers and rain, and in the raising up in v. 2. But we have already seen elsewhere that Hosea boldly uses the imagery of Baal religion in proclaiming a message from God. These verses also use language that is very much part of Hosea's message—the call to return and to know the Lord—and so the passage does not seem to be an inadequate expression of repentance. The third option above seems the best. Verses 1 and 3 begin with calls to repentance and to knowledge of God. This is certainly an exhortation or an urging. These verses are not themselves an expression of repentance but a call to express repentance. Verses 4ff. then proceed, as does the rest of the book, on the presumption that the people have not heeded the prophetic call to genuine repentance.

The chapter begins in the first person plural ("us"), and so it is clear that the prophet includes himself among the people and that the prophet is the speaker. The call is to repent, turn back to God who has torn. The word is the same as "tear" in 5:14, but there the rending is in the future; in 6:1, it has already taken place: "for it is he who has torn, and he will heal us." God is both the lion who brings punishment as discipline and the one who brings healing. The emphasis of divine judgment is clear in Hosea; it carries the purpose of instruction, of bringing the people back to God. The last line of 6:1 is a parallel: God has torn but will bandage up the wounds. The second verse also uses the imagery of healing. "After two days" and "on the third day" are parallel and suggest a brief period of time for healing, as in 2 Kings 20:5 where King Hezekiah is healed. It is possible that the verse uses the language of resurrection, as does Ezekiel 37, to speak of national recovery, but I suspect that the healing imagery is the better option. The healing will place the people in the watch and care of God, who will now be present with the people.

We have seen that in several places Hosea charges that the people have no knowledge of God. Here in v. 3, he calls the people to gain that knowledge by seeking it.

Ancient Israel is here called not to pursue lovers or Baals but to pursue a faithful relationship with God in the same way that the people are to pursue justice or peace. This genuine pursuit of knowledge leads to an encounter with God. It is as sure as the coming of each dawn; God will come to the people. The point of the rain imagery is not the surety of God's coming, for the rains were not sure in Canaan. What was sure was that the rains brought prosperity and fertility to the land and, with the crops, rejoicing to the people. Baal promised this kind of fertility, and so the prophet's use of this language is daring, but the point is that Baal does not bring the crops. God does. In this first part of chapter 6, the prophet has reflected on the difficulties of life in the northern kingdom and, in the tradition of other prophets such as Joel, Amos, or Malachi, has discerned the need for repentance. He thus calls the people to seek true knowledge of God.

An Empty National Life (6:4-11)

After Hosea's call to repentance, we find one of the most poignant verses in the book. It is often interpreted to indicate that the expression of repentance in vv. 1-3 was a false one. That view would necessitate a repentance by the people and then a further going astray for the images in the last part of v. 4 to be appropriate. I have suggested above that it is better to see vv. 1-3 as primarily connected to the last section of chapter 5 and that v. 4 of chapter 6 makes a fresh start. The short-lived love reflected in v. 4 would then refer to ancient Israel's early love of God in the wilderness, which did not last when the people entered

Canaan, or to the frequent pattern of their good intentions of faithfulness never lasting long.

> Your love is like a morning cloud,
> like the dew that goes away early.

This last section of chapter 6, then, operates under the presumption that the people are unresponsive to the prophetic cry, the presumption that undergirds the whole of the book of Hosea. God speaks in the first person in v. 4, and the picture is of the divine inner struggle with the question: What shall I do with you? The parental image comes to mind; the children, Israel and Judah, are unreliable in their relationship with the divine Parent, a Parent who does not want to send judgment their way; nonetheless, their unresponsiveness brings it upon them. Their love is like the morning cloud or dew that leaves quickly. In that part of the world, many summer days begin with an early mist that the sun quickly burns off; such is ancient Israel's loyalty in relationship with God—here today and gone tomorrow. The word for love is the same one I translated "loyalty" in 4:1. Israel's love for God as demonstrated in life has no steadfastness to it.

As a consequence of the people's desertion, God has sent prophets whose words are deadly weapons (v. 5). Elijah, Elisha, Micaiah ben Imlah, and Amos came before Hosea and also spoke words of judgment. Just as the tree is cut down, so their messages, the very words of God, strike at this people with no loyalty. The last line of v. 5 is troublesome. Does it mean that just as the prophetic word attacks the people, so does God's judgment? The problem is that something going forth as light usually carries a positive connotation in the Old Testament. We have already noted that the word for judgment here can carry the sense of justice; perhaps that sense fits best in v. 5.

Verses 4-6 may reflect a response to Hosea's proclamation that the harsh message is unjustified, especially if the people are paying great heed to their worship (v. 6), but the events described in the rest of chapter 6 certainly justify God's word of judgment, for what God desires are genuine loyalty and relationship (steadfast love and knowledge of God) far more than sacrifices. Verse 6 does not reject worship or sacrifice outright but rather speaks of priorities in religion. Worship is a response to God and an arena for God's presence with the people, not a way to obligate God to bless rather than curse. It is also clearly the prophetic view that worship relates to life, and ancient Israel's life as reflected in the remainder of chapter 6 is not a pretty sight. In any case, the worship of ancient Israel is corrupt to the very core.

The beginning of v. 7 has occasioned much debate, but the context calls for a place name, as is often the case in Hosea, rather than a reference to Adam in Genesis 3 or to humanity, which is the meaning of the Hebrew name Adam. Adam was also a place in the Jordan valley on the way to Shechem (v. 9) from Gilead (v. 8). There, according to Hosea's geography of evil, the people have broken covenant, brought alienation in their relationship with God. They have not followed the divinely-given instruction that was part of God's covenant with the people. They have demonstrated faithlessness toward God, not being trustworthy or true to the relationship. This emphasis hearkens back to the beginning of chapter 4 and God's indictment of the people who have not kept God's law that was given as covenant instruction. They commit evil, even to the point of bloodshed. There is robbery, murder, and priestly corruption. Gilead bears the footmarks of murderers. The reference may be generally to chaos in the land or refer specifically to the revolt in which Pekah seized the throne since Gilead supported that action or refer to the Assyrian attack on that area as part of the Syro-Ephraimite War.

In any of these cases, the community life of ancient Israel is now a horrible thing. Even priests commit murder like common criminals. It defiles the land, makes it unclean and thus unacceptable to God. This remarkably chaotic picture is a full demonstration of the results of adultery/idolatry in relationship with God. Even the priests who were supposed to instruct in the knowledge of God use their power and their unity to support violence. Their evil makes the land, the house of Israel, unclean or rotten. The reference in v. 10 may also include corrupt worship practices. Verses 7-10 reflect a time of conflict and bloodshed in the northern kingdom but also the failure of the people to repent in the face of such an empty and chaotic national life. Their arrogance moves them to absent God from their history. Finally, the prophet foresees the same chaos and fate for Judah.

This chapter pictures a community in which chaos is knocking at life's door, perhaps a world not so different from our own. The fundamental word of the prophet is that all the frantic efforts to deal with such chaos are doomed to failure without the resource of faith in God. This faith can bring a hope that can enable us to find our way forward.

More Emptiness (7:1–7)

The emphasis on the national life of the northern kingdom continues in chapter 7. The last line of chapter 6 likely belongs with the first verse of chapter 7 and speaks of God's restoration of the people's fortunes, of the healing of their corporate body. But when God brings good, the people do not respond with righteousness or gratitude, but with evil. Evil deeds and corruption are so ingrained in the national life that they even come to the surface at the most unreasonable time, when God has granted prosperity. The word for corruption means guilt, which has dire consequences in Hosea's proclamation. Here for the first time, Hosea uses the name of the capital of the northern kingdom, Samaria. It was an important center in the north and, in Hosea's view, a center of the people's sin. The national life was centered there, a national life filled with idolatry and with a determination to dismiss God from any consideration. This state of affairs is demonstrated with false dealings and robbery. The last line of v. 1 speaks of gangs who openly and violently rob. The import of this section is that the people leave God out of their national life, in both good times and bad.

In their neglect of God, the people have forgotten that God remembers sin and responds appropriately to it with judgment. This section probably comes from the latter years of the kingdom and the various overthrows of kings during that time, such as when Hoshea replaced Pekah on the throne. It is a time of real instability because of the deeds of the people who have left God out of their community life. Those deeds are now before God and surround the people like a flood or a besieging army.

The prophet in particular focuses on the king in the verses that follow. Verses 3-7 speak of conspirators taking advantage of a time of celebration in the royal court by initiating a revolt. The prophet then compares the conspirators to a hot oven. While the prophet took a dim view of the kings, he did not approve of the revolt because it included murder and also because kingship was divinely ordained, even if in a grudging way. (See 1 Sam 8.)

Verse 3 is difficult to interpret, but perhaps the best view is that the conspirators keep the king and his princes happy while plotting against them. They deceive the rulers, and then the prophet moves to his comparison with the hot oven. The oven is one used primarily to bake bread, a clay oven; archaeologists have discovered several examples. The prophet continues the image with an account of the professional baker who would normally stir the coals occasionally to bring the hot coals to the top, but at night would sleep and leave the oven unattended and the dough would rise. The fire would then die down, but the oven would remain hot to the touch. The conspirators in the intrigue do not appear to burn with opposition to the king but are nonetheless hot to overthrow him; they are deceptive.

The day of the king (v. 5) refers to the day of his accession, or its anniversary, or to his birthday, or, perhaps more to the point in this case, to the day of the king's death, which is about to commence in the revolt. The overthrow proceeds with getting the king's officials and supporters, princes, drunk so that their opposition is of no consequence. The last line of v. 5 is difficult; perhaps it means that the king joins in with the princes who are drunk, but it could be translated to mean that the power of the wine inflames the renegades. Still the revolt continues.

The prophet returns to the simile of the oven in vv. 6-7. The text is difficult in the first line of v. 6; it could simply be "they draw near; they lie in wait." But NRSV's translation of their hearts burning like an oven with intrigue is also plausible. In any case, the plot is afoot. The remainder of the verse conjures up the image of the baker sleeping and allowing the coals in the oven to smolder at night and then upon stirring them in the morning, they flame up. Thus it is with the conspirators' anger; it festers for a night but attack comes with the morning.

The figure of the oven continues in v. 7; the conspirators all glow with anger and devour their rulers. "Rulers" is a general term for political leaders and would have included the king. It is the word used for "judges," but political and judicial leaders were generally considered together in Israel. "All their kings have fallen" looks back on the history of the northern kingdom and its instability. Kings were removed by plot and assassination. This verse may reflect the several *coups* that took place during the life of Hosea. Perhaps the murder of Pekah and subsequent crowning of Hoshea occasioned such comment. The last line of v. 7 is the most telling for Hosea. Even in this setting of national crisis and instability, the community prefers to trust in foreign alliances rather than God. The picture of life in the northern kingdom is not a very attractive one. The prosecutor continues to display the evidence. To follow the prophet's lead, their religion is half-baked.

Trust in Alliances (7:8–16)

The rest of the chapter continues the emphasis on the nation's political life, but especially emphasizes their trust in alliances with other nations. That emphasis corresponds well with the previous topic of the overthrow of kings for those plots often related closely to foreign policy. A new king brought a new foreign policy, and ideed that foreign policy concern may have led to the plot, especially with reference to Assyria. The issue for Hosea is not so much a particular foreign policy but how foreign policy reveals the condition of the community.

The prophet continues in v. 8 to use the baking image of the first part of the chapter. Now the people are not distinctively the people of God but simply an ingredient to be mixed with others. They have become a failed cake, that is burned on one side and uncooked on the other. As a culinary delight, they are not appealing to anyone. Politically, the foreign alliances in which Israel has entered have only served to sap the nation's strength. The people believed these alliances strengthened them, but in fact they drained the kingdom's resources; for example, they had paid tribute to Assyria, and Tiglath-Pileser III took territory from them. The gray hair of age is often spoken of in honorific terms in the Old Testament, but here it speaks of the loss of the strength of youth; gray hair is thrown in among Israel's other hair color. Foreign powers drain the strength of Israel, and the people do not even know it. Once again, Israel lacks knowledge. The repetition of the line is for emphasis. Even with the drain Assyria places on the nation, they think nothing has changed politically and certainly not religiously.

That theme continues in v. 10, the opening line of which also occurs at 5:5 in a context that emphasizes that the people do not know and do not repent (5:4). The conclusion of the first section of chapter 7 (v. 7) also indicates that the people do not respond to God. Israel's stubbornness and arrogance testify against them in their trial. In a way reminiscent of Amos 4, the prophet is astonished at the lack of awareness that they need to repent, even in the face of all that has happened to them. The verse gives particular emphasis to the lack of repentance.

The use of imagery continues in v. 11 with the comparison of a dove to the behavior of Israel; they have changed and become like a dove flitting all around. Their behavior is like that of the foolish person in Proverbs, the one who has never learned about life and so does not know how to act wisely. The image of the dove fits well Israel's flitting back and forth between Egypt and Assyria. In the latter years of their history, Israel did flip flops in foreign policy, alternately submitting to Assyria and asserting independence with the encouragement of Egypt. We have already noted that the northern kingdom was a prized geographical possession. In a sense Assyria and Egypt competed for Israel's loyalty and the nation itself wandered back and forth between the two. Note that v. 11 says they "call upon Egypt," instead of calling upon God (v. 7). As Israel is a bird, so now God will hunt the kingdom like a bird. As the bird flies back and forth, the hunter will spread the net and catch the people and bring them down like a hunted bird. In a different way, God will now block Israel from pursuing other loyalties as God blocked the people with a wall from pursuing other lovers in 2:6-7.

The translation of the last line of v. 12 is problematic. NRSV probably gets at the point but not the image of the Hebrew. It continues to speak of the hunter's capturing birds when they flock about. The point is that God will interrupt these incessant appeals to foreign powers, for they are sapping the internal life of the community.

Verse 13 presses the matter in quite straight-forward terms.

> Woe to them, for they have strayed from me!
> Destruction to them, for they have rebelled against me!
> I would redeem them, but they speak lies against me.

The matter is not a simple or small one, for the people have abandoned God, rebelled against God, and thus destruction is prophesied for them. Note the contrast: God would redeem, rescue them from Assyrian domination or other military threat, but Israel is defiant. What are the lies with which God is falsely accused? The reference is probably to the people's lack of trust that God can help in their national life, and so they keep flocking to foreign political powers.

It is easy for readers of an English translation to miss the significance of the first word of v. 13, "Woe." The word indicates that the prophet is already grieving over the destruction God will bring because of the rebellion of Israel. The destruction, from the point of view of the speaker, is already considered an accomplished fact, and the prophet speaks a dirge for the people.

The people continue to cry out, even using God's name, but the cries are not genuine and in that sense also demonstrate rebellion. It is clear that the cries are not genuine because of their actions. The beds from which they cry are probably the places of the sexual rituals used to secure prosperity in the nature fertility religions. They also mutilate (gash) themselves, apparently a custom associated with idol worship. It is prohibited in Deuteronomy 14:1, and the prophets of Baal gashed themselves in the contest with Elijah on Mount Carmel described in 1 Kings 18. This custom was apparently part of the ritual to seek help; it at least seeks prosperity, the grain and wine the fertility religions offered (v. 14).

Verse 15 again emphasizes the contrast between God's provision and Israel's rebellion. God has provided military training for the people, but they still turn away and seek to replace God with an idol. The conclusion of the chapter makes clear that the prophet speaks of more than an inept foreign policy; he speaks of the adultery/idolatry of the people. Their national policy constitutes rebellion against God. As the marginal note in NRSV indicates, the beginning of v. 16 is difficult, but a reference to Baal fits the context well. That is, after all, the real problem in Israel, and their political life provides the evidence. They are not faithful to their identity, and so their leaders fall in battle. Israel is "like a defective bow," either a bow that does not shoot straight and so misses the target or a bow with archers who turn and run in the heat of battle. (See Psalm 78:57.) They fall from the cursing of their tongue, the exaggerated rejection of Hosea's message by the leaders. Their downfall will prompt derision, ridicule, in Egypt, the place they sought help.

In 1-2 Kings, kings are evaluated on two bases—faithfulness to true worship of God in the temple and a foreign policy that is above all a demonstration of faith in God. The connection between foreign policy and faith is also at the forefront in Hosea 7. God is concerned about the whole of the life of ancient Israel, including political life. Faith is the bedrock of every dimension of life.

Questions for Reflection

1. What is the governing metaphor of chapters 4-11? Who is on trial? Who is the judge? Who is the jury?
2. What is the result of a lack of the "knowledge of God?"
3. Why does Hosea so severely criticize the religious leaders? Why does the king come under judgment?
4. What was the background of the Syro-Ephraimite War?
5. How do you interpret Hosea 6:1-3?
6. Why did Israel form foreign alliances? Why was this practice displeasing to the prophet?
7. How is the political instability of the last years of the northern kingdom reflected in the book of Hosea?

Chapter 3

The Law Suit (Part II)

Hosea 8–11

In the face of God's passionate love,
the prophet is haunted by the scandal of Israel's desertion.

—Abraham Heschel
The Prophets

Further Accusation (8:1–3)

Chapter 8 brings together a variety of accusations against the people to further God's indictment. Verses 1-3 form an introductory section in which God commands the prophet to raise an alarm at the coming of an enemy attack. For contemporary readers, the translation "a vulture is over the house" may be misleading. The bird is either a vulture or eagle, and the translation "one like a vulture/eagle comes against the house" may be a better rendition. So the picture of Israel as a corpse with the vulture circling may not be present. The figure rather connotes the swiftness of the invader, as is fitting with v. 3.

The house of the Lord usually refers to a sanctuary. Perhaps that is where the prophet is speaking or perhaps that is the good luck charm in which the people Israel have come to trust. The reason for the enemy at the door is that the people have broken or violated the covenant. While the term here refers primarily to the Mosaic covenant, the agreed relationship between God and Israel concluded at Sinai, the prophet's language may also bring to mind the international treaties Israel has not kept as part of their political flip-flopping in the latter years of their national history. The use of "my law" as a parallel to covenant makes clear the primary referent, however. The prophet is talking about God's instruction or teaching or guidance or will that was part of the instruction in how to live as God's people. Covenant and law are of a piece, and it is that against which the people have rebelled. We have already noted the reference in Deuteronomy 33:10 to the effect that the priests are to teach God's instruction. (See also Deuteronomy 31:9-13.) They have not only neglected this task, but even led the people in rebellion.

In this time of trial, the people turn to God, but their words are false, indeed arrogant. They claim to know God; they may know about God, but the prophet has already pronounced in no uncertain terms that Israel has no knowledge of God. They do not have a relationship with God, and they do not have a proper view of God. Again in arrogance and self-assurance, Israel has spurned Yahweh. They have also rejected that which is morally good for all, and thus the enemy pursues the kingdom. The enemy is probably not God here, for God is speaking, but the enemy attacking is a result of the corrupt and foolish life of the people. The first three verses have introduced this set of accusations in a general way; now the accusations will become more specific.

Political Charges (8:4–10)

The threat that begins with v. 4 has to do with the unauthorized changing of political leadership. The prophet assumes that kings were to be ordained of God, and presumably the princes came with a new king. They were the officials closest to the king. The nation as a whole has left God out of its political life, as illustrated in the variety of revolts and counter-revolts in the last years of the northern kingdom. The use of "knowledge" is interesting in v. 4. Now it is God who has no knowledge, for the people have not consulted him.

The next charge is that the people have manufactured idols. Remember that in 2:8 we have already heard of using silver and gold for Baal, and also remember that the first king of the northern kingdom of Israel, Jeroboam I, set up sanctuaries with golden calves at Bethel and Dan. Here again, king and idolatry are linked, idolatry that is clearly prohibited in the Ten Commandments. The point of the graven image of the god was that it gave a fixed point of contact with the divine. No doubt, in Canaan that was an attempt to help worshipers make the god tangible, but the problem is that the fixed point of contact, the image, could be moved, manipulated, used by the worshipers; it could simply be picked up (Jer 10:5). Thus comes the temptation to manipulate the god, or God in the case of the Hebrews, and so graven images are prohibited. The God of ancient Israel was not to be manipulated; God initiated a relationship with ancient Israel and asked in response fidelity to that relationship. There are consequences for rebellion, destruction, perhaps both for idols and people (v. 4).

The calf spurned in v. 5 is probably that of Bethel, a place Hosea speaks of harshly elsewhere; Samaria, the capital as a symbol of the people as a whole, would have close ties to Bethel and Dan. Some have suggested that there was a golden calf or young bull in a sanctuary in Samaria. The golden calf may have been intended to be a graven image of God or a visible symbol of the presence of God. Either way, the image leaned toward the idol worship of Baalism and encouraged the people down that path. Hosea rejects any such idolatry. The last part of v. 5 has God speaking a complaint in the tradition of the lament psalms such as Psalm 13: How long will it be until Israel is innocent? The charge of idolatry continues in v. 6, and reflects the prophetic ridiculing of the idols we noted in 4:12. The image cannot be God, a superior being, because it was made by human hands. The destruction of the calf will show that the idol is but a human work. The image was likely a piece of wood covered with silver and gold, and it would be smashed.

Verse 7 gives the reason for the judgment pronounced upon the people and does so with two proverbial sayings that were probably known in Hosea's time. The first saying is familiar and affirms the connection between acts and consequences for the people. There is a moral sense to life. Sowing trouble brings trouble. The saying may well imply that the use of the calf (v. 6) is sowing the wind. The life of the people brings consequences but apparently consequences different from those the people expect. They will reap the whirlwind. The second saying suggests that one

can predict the harvest by inspecting the grain. The waywardness of the people is plain to see, and its consequences sure in time. In this saying, the words for "heads" and "meal" rhyme, an unusual device in Hebrew. The last line of the verse makes the point in certain terms. Harvest trouble is at hand, and even if harvest comes, the people will not benefit from it for foreign oppressors will take it. This verse is a rather dire prophecy for a people heavily involved in religious practices designed to bring fertility.

The prophet continues to press the consequences, and v. 8 allows a shift back to a more explicit emphasis on the political, especially foreign policy. The image is of a dish from which everything has been eaten and only the dish remains. They have nothing to offer in foreign alliances now; they must now pay tribute to attract allies, which previously Hosea has likened to lovers. Again, one can see the condition of the nation by observing its life. They are now but another nation to be used. There may be further significance here. When Israel came out of Egypt, God had designated the people as a special divine treasure, "my treasured possession out of all peoples," but now they are simply another nation to be had. Such a state of affairs is the result of living not as people of God but as people of Baal.

The image in v. 9 could refer to the wildness of Ephraim in seeking foreign alliances such as in Assyria, but with the phrase "wandering alone," the image is likely of a wandering refugee with nowhere to go and no friends, lost and forlorn Ephraim needing to hire lovers. The background would appear to be Assyrian invasion and destruction. This section contains stinging images. Here the prostitute Ephraim must pay clients. Rather than clients' paying the prostitute and bringing profit, the prostitute must, in a real reversal, pay clients. Israel sought to pay for Assyria's allegiance but it will be to no avail; it cannot protect the people from the divine judgment. God will bring the kingdom's political life to an end. The picture in

v. 10 is of a disciplinary judgment very much in line with the picture of Gomer's judgment in chapter 3. Hosea prophesies that God will now gather the "wandering" people for judgment and bring an end to their wayward political shenanigans.

Judgment on an Empty Life (8:11–14)

The primary emphasis of this last section of chapter 8 is a preoccupation with sacrifice rather than obedience. We have already seen this theme, but the last verse also points to trust in militarism. Political and religious dimensions of life are intertwined. Verses 13-14 both end with firm words of judgment. Verse 11 speaks of a real irony. The place ("altars") intended for the removal of sin has become the place for increasing sin. The sinful people have built more places of worship, and that worship has become the center of their disobedience.

The prophet continues with the theme of multiplying in this chapter, a chapter full of masterful examples of the artful use of language. The people ignore God's instruction as we have seen before; they have no knowledge of God, for the priests have not instructed them in it. Even if God's laws were multiplied, they would be so unfamiliar to the people as to be called strange. The laws referred to could be the Ten Commandments since Hosea reflects familiarity with that code. Rather than obedience, the people love sacrifice, and they especially love eating the meat from the offerings. The people's attitude is reminiscent of Saul's attitude in 1 Samuel 15, where Samuel reminds the king that obedience takes priority over sacrifice (1 Sam 15:22-23). The usual way of saying that God accepts the sacrifices is to say that God delights in them, but these sacrifices God rejects, no matter how much pleasure they may bring the people. God will remember their iniquity and punish the sin of the people, a part of which is false sacrifice. The bondage that is their punishment will amount to a reversal of their history. They will go back to slavery in Egypt.

We noted at the end of chapter 7 the expectation that some will be exiled to Egypt; here the reversal of Israel's history makes the prophecy even more powerful. This prophecy calls to mind the name of the third child in chapter 1—Lo-ammi ("Not my people") "for you are not my people and I am not your God." The breaking of covenant brings the further reversal of exile in Egypt.

The final charge in this chapter is that Israel has placed trust in palaces and fortifications rather than in its maker. They have forgotten their maker, again a lack of knowledge. The theme of mutiplying continues. They have built palaces, often strongly armed and fortified cities. The chapter concludes with a clear word of jugment very similar to those in the oracles of judgment on the nations in Amos 1-2. Destruction is at hand for these cities in which Israel trusts for protection. The "strongholds" were special fortified parts of buildings, probably the possessions of royalty or the leading citizens of the realm. The image of fire pictures the divine wrath. This chapter has thus listed Israel's sin as a part of God's indictment against them in this law suit. The evidence is overpowering: a political life that ignores God's sovereignty, the making of images, a woeful foreign policy, an emphasis on sacrifice rather than obedience, and a trust in fortifications rather than God.

An End to Worship (9:1–9)

This section focuses on worship and was probably delivered at a major sanctuary in the northern kingdom, perhaps Bethel. The prophet proclaims a coming judgment of exile that will center on an end to the enjoyment of the fruits of the land and an end to the ability to celebrate festivals. It could well be that the prophet here interrupts the celebration of the Feast of Tabernacles that was observed in the autumn at Bethel. The prophecy articulates the reversal of ancient Israel's salvation history, a theme we have seen as recently as 8:13. This proclamation seems to have received a hostile response (v. 7), reminiscent of the response to Amos from the priest Amaziah at Bethel (Amos 7:10-17).

The chapter begins with the prophet addressing the people with a call to non-praise. It is a clear reversal of the call to praise that begins the hymns of praise in the Psalter. (See, for example, Ps 117:1.) The reason given for not praising is the one characteristic of Hosea: Israel's adultery /idolatry. They have played the part of the prostitute and gone after Baal. The time of reckoning has come, and there is now no place for rejoicing in this festival. Israel's praise is to cease, a praise Hosea characterizes as on a par with that of other idolatrous nations.

Some have suggested that threshing floors may have been one of the places the sexual rites of Baal were enacted, but it may simply be that the grain being threshed was part of the "fertility" sought in the Canaanite religion; that would explain the reference at the end of v. 1 and fit the context of v. 2. The great festivals of Israel's worship had the purpose of ensuring fertility in the land. Now the prophet proclaims that the people will go into exile and not enjoy the fruits of the land and not experience festival worship.

These themes are all bound together in this first part of chapter 9. God is no longer their shepherd to feed them, a reversal of another psalm of praise, Psalm 23, a psalm of trust. The harvests, represented with the threshing floor, winevat, and new wine, which the fertility religion promises, will fail. Exile shall come. Verse 3 is a clear prophecy of that. Because of Israel's adultery/idolatry, the people face eviction from the land, for the land belongs to God and the people have rejected God's presence and rule. We have noted earlier references to a return to Egypt, but here there is also prophecy of exile to Assyria. Because in Assyria idol worship pervaded all of life, the food there would be unclean. Exile will be difficult for a people who are more interested in observing ritualism than faithfulness to God. It was common imperial policy for the Assyrians to deport conquered peoples. They were harsh conquerors and often replaced their captives with those from other nations. That is what happened with the northern kingdom, and the intermingling of the remnant of Samaria (Israel) with those from other nations produced the Samaritans of New Testament times.

Having introduced the coming judgment, the prophet presses the charges further in v. 4. Sacrifice will no longer be offered to God; indeed, in Assyria/Egypt, it will probably have to be offered to the local sovereign. Libations of wine were apparently offered with sacrifice (Exod 29:40-41), but there will be no more sacrifice to God.

The emphasis on uncleanness continues. Mourners' bread was that eaten in a house where there had been a death, and thus the bread and other items there were infected by the contagious uncleanness of the corpse. (Corpses were unclean because death was an enemy of God.) Those who eat of that bread will also be defiled; such will also be Israel's fate in exile. The emphasis on uncleanness shows that the prophet Hosea was very much aware of priestly tradition and its importance as part of God's covenant instruction. Bread that is defiled by death cannot be used in sacrifices in the sanctuary (Deut 26:14); those in mourning cannot worship; their bread is only for satisfying the physical need of hunger. Israel will go into exile and be like that, excluded from worship and thus from the community of God's people.

All of this fits well the setting of a festival in which the people would bring the fruits of the land to the sanctuary, and Hosea startles them by interrupting with this strong word of judgment. Then, in lightning fashion, he asks, "What will you do on the day of this festival in exile? You will be in Assyria and Egypt and the place in Israel where you have had your life and your idols will be overgrown." The particular festival may have been the Feast of Tabernacles, but the three special festivals, the Feast of Tabernacles, Passover, and Pentecost, which necessitated pilgrimage to a sanctuary were likely included in his prophecy, for the sanctuaries would not be there to host them. Death will come in exile. Memphis was once a capital of the Egyptian empire and of particular importance were its burial sites. Egypt will gather Israel for death and burial, at the important burial place of Memphis.

Israel's day of reckoning because of their great sin is upon them, and they shall know it. They lack knowledge in so many ways, but the judgment will be so clear that even this people without knowledge will know it. The second half of v. 7 indicates that Hosea was called a fool and mad man, perhaps the common way of the day to discount the irrelevant babblings of those who claimed to be prophets. The fool was one who knew nothing and was not worthy of being heard, but Hosea's word of judgment comes because of the sin of Israel.

The people's hostile response to the prophet continues in v. 8 where Hosea reminds his audience that the prophet was to be guardian of the people. The reference to Gibeah in v. 9 brings to mind the well-known succession of atrocities in Judges 19-21, a time of great evil. That is how corrupt Ephraim is now.

A Barren Future (9:10–17)

The pressing of God's indictment against the people in the middle part of the book from chapter 4 on has contained powerful, eloquent words of judgment. Israel does not stand well as a defendant. The book makes something of a shift from 9:10 through chapter 11. The trial is still at hand, but the prophet refers more often to the hopeful traditions of Israel's salvation history, though he often does so for the purpose of showing that God's future for the people includes judgment. The prophecies are reminiscent of chapter 2. Verse 10 illustrates this tendency.

> Like grapes in the wilderness,
>   I found Israel.
> Like the first fruit on the fig tree,
>   in its first season,
>   I saw your ancestors.
> But they came to Baal-Peor,
>   and consecrated themselves to a

thing of shame,
and became detestable like the
thing they loved.

A traveler in the wilderness would be delighted to come upon grapes, and the first fruits of a fig tree were especially tender. God greatly delighted in Israel when the people came out of bondage in Egypt, but then they came to Baal-Peor, as described in Numbers 25. Already the seduction of Canaanite fertility religion was evident, even as they prepared to enter the land. The people have become detestable like the thing they worship. Heavy irony is in the prophet's voice as the words "consecrated themselves" were often used of the special consecration of the people to God. The people have forsaken God, and thus God's delight in them is no more.

The remainder of the chapter speaks in no uncertain terms of the barren future the people face. Ephraim's glory shall fly away, and thus there will be no children born. The glory might refer to the splendor, might, and power of Ephraim, but the conclusion of v. 12 may indicate that Ephraim's glory is God. Glory is a manifestation of God's presence and activity in the world; when God is not present, a fruitful future is not possible. All of these images of fruitfulness and barrenness once again represent Hosea's bold use of the language of the fertility religion of the day as a way to proclaim God's message to a people bound by that fertility religion. The future with that religion only offers infertility: no conception, no pregnancy, no birth. Even those who are born will be cut down; the funeral dirge of "woe" is upon them. The children of Israel will be hunted, will go to battle to be cut down. The slaughter is clear and painful. In an ironic shift, barrenness is suddenly seen as a gift from God in v. 14 because if a child is born, it will only suffer. The only way to avoid death is barrenness.

With v. 15, God again refers to the beginning of the alienation in the relationship with Israel, an alienation that brings barrenness. The reference to Gilgal is significant. There Saul's kingship began, and the verse concludes with a reference to rulers, so the prophet may well be commenting on the evil of the monarchy in Israel. But Gilgal was also a place of worship, and the verse contains reference to a sanctuary, "my house." So both political and sacrificial sins are in view, and because of their multitude of sins, God will love them no more, a phrase reminiscent of the name of the second child in chapter 1, Lo-ruhamah, "Not pitied." Like a dead fruit tree, Israel is stricken from the root up and thus can bear no fruit. No future, only judgment is at hand. In Genesis 41:52, the name Ephraim is derived from a Hebrew word meaning to be fruitful. Here Ephraim has become precisely the opposite—barren. The concluding verse in the chapter makes their future clear; it was, in fact, no future at all, and therein was God's judgment. The future is wandering among the nations, in exile and trouble.

The images in this last section of chapter 9 are striking. They were, no doubt, even more pointed in Hosea's time. The poem is sad and moving. A number of readers will be bothered by the language of these verses that speaks of God's hating the people and not loving them anymore and casting them off and even cutting them down. The powerful imagery is characteristic of prophetic words of judgment. We need to remember that the prophetic word of judgment was, in fact, a word unto salvation and not a word unto condemnation. It had the purpose of calling the people to faithfulness in their relationship with God, for therein and therein only is wholeness of life to be found.

I suspect that Grady Nutt was right when he suggested that it is hard for us to hear these words. We tend to hear them as if we were the hot dog on the straightened wire hanger being held over the fire and burned to a crisp. We hear them as negative words calling our very selves into question. The images and words in chapter 9 are harsh, but Hosea's times demanded harsh words. His task was to awaken the people to the death-giving way they were living. His words are designed to bring the people back to faith in God. The words are in that sense polemic and must be read as having that exaggerated quality about them. The God who sends this message by Hosea is no wishy-washy God, but a tough God, the same kind of powerful God of which Jesus spoke in the Gospels, for the people in Hosea's audience needed tough love. They will not come to healing with a pat on the head and a reassurance that all will be well. All will not be well. Their national life is fundamentally rotten, and unless they deal with their faithlessness, they have no future. That house divided with murder, robbery, lying, and adultery cannot stand. God wishes them to have life and so screams for them to choose life, to choose blessing found in faithful relationship with God.

Politics and Worship (10:1–8)

The first half of chapter 10 combines themes now familiar to the reader of Hosea. The passage begins and ends with altars, pillars (idols), and high places, but very much interwoven in the text is the futility of the monarchy. No doubt the king was in control of worship in the northern kingdom, and it operated to the aid of the royal court. The king also sought to guarantee prosperity for the nation, including national security, and the worship of the day espoused the same purpose. So the themes are related in the life of the community. The passage builds artfully with accusation leading toward an announcement of judgment. The people again believed that the system was the solution, and so they, no doubt when they enjoyed the crowning of new kings such as Pekah and Hoshea, once again believed that king and worship would succeed. But Hosea knew otherwise; Assyria would keep coming back; king and worship were scheduled for destruction. Perhaps then the people would come to faith. In order for Hosea to function as a prophet and in order for his words to be preserved, he had to have supporters, often called disciples or a school. Because this text speaks of the people in the third person ("they"), perhaps he spoke these words to his supporters as significant interpretation of the times.

The chapter begins with a striking figure--Israel as a luxuriant vine. The image of Israel as a vine that grows is a traditional one. (See Ps 80.) The vine prospered but then misused the prosperity. With growth, more altars were added—plowing investment back into the business. More altars would mean more prosperity. Also improved were the pillars, apparently representative of a god or an ancestor in Canaanite worship and prohibited in Exodus 23:24 and 34:13 and Deuteronomy 16:22. Those altars and pillars would be broken. Again, Hosea's language is daring and ironic, perhaps even offensive. The verb used is the one for breaking the neck of an animal used in sacrifice; now sacrifice will be broken because the people are deceptive.

With this stinging beginning to the passage, the prophet moves to the king. Now the judgment is upon the people, and they realize that the king is powerless to help. The prophet speaks of the disillusionment that will come with the plundering of king and sanctuaries. Perhaps the coming judgment can bring the people to some kind of knowledge. At least they may recognize that they have no fear of God, that is reverence, awe, respect for God. "Fear" is similar to knowledge of God. It connotes obedience more than cowardice.

The first part of v. 4 probably continues from v. 3 to describe the actions of the kings: empty words, oaths, and covenants. Consequently, rather than the desired result of prosperity and safety, what grows in the fields is the poisonous weeds of conflict. The prophet looks forward to an Assyrian invasion and continues to speak of the reaction of the people. They now tremble, fearful that the failure of the political system will bring the destruction of the place of worship and the calf at Bethel or, as Hosea calls it, Beth-aven, "House of evil." People and priest will mourn its destruction.

The last line of v. 5 contains irony. God's glory departs and thus Israel is destroyed, but their mourning is over the glory that has departed from their idolatrous sanctuary, the golden calf. This mourning shows that the people are no longer God's people, as indicated in the name of the third child in chapter 1. Even the golden calf will go the way of tribute to the great Assyrian king, and Israel will see that both their political and religious plans have brought only trouble.

The prophet then boldly declares that the king in Samaria will perish in helplessness. He will fall as a twig sinks from the surface of a lake. With the last verse in this section, the prophet returns to his beginning point. King will fall, and so will the corrupt places of worship in the kingdom. The two go together. The section concludes by returning to the altars, pillars, and high places. The collapse of political life will also mean the collapse of the worship centers. We have already had occasion to refer to the high places in chapters 4 and 10, places made for sacrifice. They came to symbolize the mixing of Baalism into the faith of Israel. "Aven" means evil, and thus the high places of evil may be the various places of worship throughout the land. "Aven" may also be short for Beth-aven, Hosea's derogatory euphemism for Bethel. The sin of Israel is here characterized as being related to worship, and the result is that the altars of the land will be forsaken and abandoned and overgrown. Just as in 9:6, dwellings and idols will be overgrown, so also will the altars.

In 4:13, the mountains and hills were places of sacrifice and not spoken of positively. In another reversal, here the people call to the mountains and hills for help. "They" probably refers to the people rather than the altars. The cry is for deliverance from the coming devastation; the people sense that to be buried by mountains and hills will be a better fate than facing the invaders. The prophet in this section has provided a clear glimpse of the condition of the people. King and worship are intertwined, and both are corrupted by the ideology of Baalism. Their religion has become a syncretistic one. What they have put in place to ensure peace and prosperity will in actuality bring only destruction.

Proclamation of War (10:9–15)

The remainder of chapter 10 speaks of the coming war as judgment on Israel. The prophet has already referred to

Gibeah and the gross sin described in Judges 19-21. Those events again become the type to which Israel's current condition is compared. In those chapters, a Levite's concubine is abused by a mob in Gibeah and left for dead. The tribes are then called to war against Gibeah in the land of Benjamin to deal with this outrageous violation of the custom of hospitality, and much bloodshed follows. The story is a gruesome one that the shapers of Judges cite as a prime illustration that the people are in a dark and chaotic time before the establishing of the monarchy. Hosea says that Israel has sinned from Gibeah on and is still in that state. Just as in Judges, war will follow the sin, but here not just the tribes will gather for combat; other nations will gather. The people were familiar with the tradition of God's coming to bless. Here the prophet ties a declaration of war with God's coming, for God comes against the people, people who are wayward and have gone astray. The purpose of this judging presence is chastisement, the disciplining punishment we have seen before in Hosea. The nations will gather against them to attack, to chastise, the people for their double iniquity, perhaps the iniquity of the time of Gibeah and the iniquity of the present.

The theme continues in the next verses that introduce agricultural metaphors to make their point. First, the people are compared to a trained heifer (v. 11). The comparison is similar to the one in 4:16 that spoke of the disobedience of the people, and here it has the purpose of contrasting Israel's initial willingness to obey God with the current rebellious attitude. God had not made Israel to pull heavy loads initially, but now with the sin of the people, Ephraim/Israel will be put to the yoke and made to do hard labor. A harder and unrewarding task now comes as the prophet makes a broad announcement of judgment.

The threat is not only for the northern kingdom but also for Judah, the southern kingdom. The whole of the people will be put to the yoke. This is apparently the point of the reference to Jacob whose name was changed to Israel in Genesis 32. The future of hard labor is for the whole of the people.

The prophet then continues the use of agricultural images in v. 12, but now Israel is the farmer, the sower rather than the animal, and the prophet uses exhortation rather than a pronouncement of judgment. He urges the people to faithfulness. The prophet used the image of sowing and reaping in 8:7 in a negative way to describe the empty life of Israel; here the exhortation is to sow in righteousness and reap according to unchanging love. We have seen these terms before. They carry ethical implications. To sow in righteousness is to live in right relationship, in fidelity to relationship with God. The issue is not always doing the right moral act in a legalistic sense, but a lifestyle based in faithfulness, fidelity to a relationship that God has initiated. Human relationships of integrity issue from this basis. The people will then reap according to steadfast love. This word includes love, mercy, grace, constancy, loyalty. By living a righteous life one finds God's constant love.

This interpretation assumes that the love is of divine rather than human origin. The people are then called to attend to what they have not, to plow their fallow ground, a symbol of repentance, or reorientation of life. The next line describes it as seeking the Lord. Thus the prophet calls the people to repentance now, as at the end of chapter 5 and beginning of chapter 6. The call is to repentance, not the casual, corrupt worship typical of the day but an act of genuine penitence in the midst of crisis. The prophet then promises a return of God to rain righteousness or salvation upon the people. It is important to understand that the call to repentance is not a call to earn salvation but to make a life-changing decision to act on the basis of the promise of God's constancy and love. Therein is hope.

The people, however, have not done thus, and the last three verses of chapter 10 return to the pressing of God's indictment against the people and accompanying words of judgment. The people have not plowed in righteousness, but have plowed iniquity and thus reap injustice. They have practiced deception in human relationships, in political matters, in international diplomacy, and in their worship. The particular charge here is trust in military power, in chariots and armies. The northern kingdom had a reputation and thus pride in their military, especially their chariots, and, no doubt, the kings led the people to trust in militarism. So corresponding to the sin of militarism and in line with the emphasis begun in v. 9, the prophet then declares that war is at hand and that the fortifications of Israel will fall.

The prophet then illustrates the prophecy with a well-known atrocity of that era. Just as Shalman destroyed Beth-arbel in which both mother and children were brutally murdered, so shall Israel be destroyed. Shalman could be a form of Salamanu, a Moabite ruler of the time, but more likely a form of the Assyrian ruler's name Shalmaneser. The identification of Beth-arbel is problematic but may well be a town in the north, in Galilee. The future holds barrenness as in chapter 9 and even cruel atrocities. The conclusion of the chapter emphasizes the fall of the king in Samaria in the coming war, a time of profound crisis. The fall will come quickly, and God will not rescue the king. Samaria fell to the Assyrians in precisely this way. It was

cut off, besieged, and the king was trapped. Plowing injustice reaps woe.

God's Love and Israel's Lack of Response (11:1-11)

This chapter brings the lengthy middle section of the book to a crescendo. It continues to press the accusation against the people and refers to the salvation-history of the people and makes use of moving images. It also offers a word of hope. The chapter begins with accusation and judgment, all put in stark contrast to the history of God's gracious deliverance of the people. God's history is a gracious one, Israel's a sinful one. Defeat, exile, and death come from Israel's history. The contrast between God's history of gracious acts toward the people and the sin of Israel in Hosea's time highlights the sin of the people, but God cannot abandon the child even though the prophetic message of judgment remains. The time of punishment has an end. The judgment will be a disciplining, a refining one, one of instruction or chastisement, a word we have already seen in Hosea.

The chapter begins with a moving image of the parent loving the child and raising and nurturing the child only to be rejected by the child. Many parents will be able to identify with the emotional baggage of this image. The reference is back to the historical tradition of the deliverance from Egypt, the Exodus, and of God's care for the child Israel at an early age. The traditions centering on the Exodus from Egypt were apparently held in high regard and preserved especially in the northern kingdom. God's word called the people out of slavery in Egypt, and God continued to call to the people through the prophets. The tender heavenly Parent cared for the child. Nonethelesss, upon entering Canaan, idolatry began. This is made explicit in the last line of v. 2: sacrificing to idols, Baalism. The poignant figure of speech continues in vv. 3-4. The Parent has taught the child to walk, held the child close to the breast, but despite this nurturing and help, the child Israel did not know the divine Parent. We have already from 2:8 on seen that Israel does not know; we might say the child is clueless.

They did not know the divine physician. The healing (v. 3) refers to the times in their history when God has rescued the people from crisis. The people's lack of knowledge here has a specific historical point. Throughout their history, God has restored the people from times of weakness. Hosea has referred to the stories in Judges on occasion; there the people got into trouble because of disobedience, but God raised up leaders (judges) to deliver them. The prophet's point is that despite all this care from the Parent throughout life, the child Israel does not know or realize that it is God who has made possible this recovery. The leading in v. 4 is more a drawing, a wooing if you will, with the pull of compassion, an inducement suitable for humans rather than animals. God has not forced Israel with real harnesses, but has sought to draw the people with love. God, as the kind farmer, has indeed eased the yoke to give the people rest for a time from their burden. The divine Parent has also bent down to them, perhaps to hear them, and fed them repeatedly in their history. God especially fed the people in the wilderness, but the food from the land of Canaan is also the provision of God, a particularly pressing point in Hosea's setting. God has held the child close and nurtured the child, but to no avail.

The picture of God in this touching passage is one parents can appreciate. It is traditionally described as God the Father, an image entirely appropriate to the Old Testament, but the tasks of parenthood described are ones that include those traditionally assigned to mothers. The child is called "my son" after the figure Jacob/Israel in Genesis, but the picture of God is more inclusive than gender specific. The image is of a tender, caring, compassionate God whose love for Israel has been slighted but not extinguished. The prophet calls the readers to expand rather than limit their images of God.

Because Israel has spurned God's love, exile is at hand. Verse 5 is similar to others in Hosea, but the change from the tender image of God's love in v. 4 is startling, and that would appear to be the intention. The contrast between God's love and the people's sin is put in full view. Exile to Egypt and Assyria Hosea has prophesied in several passages. The journey to Egypt is a return to bondage, and Assyria will lord it over Israel. Note the word play: They will *return* to Egypt because they refused to *return* to God; indeed v. 2 says they kept turning away from God. The coming exile will be the result of a military invasion by the Assyrians. The kingdom of ancient Israel practiced deceit in their foreign policy, and their flirting with Egypt to bring about an anti-Assyrian alliance for the purpose of asserting independence will bring the brunt of the cruel Assyrian military juggernaut to bear against the kingdom. Thus the sword will whirl against the people, and conquer their cities.

> The sword rages in their cities,
> it consumes their oracle-priests,
> and devours because of their schemes.

The reference is to the arrogant and boastful politicians of the day, those who use empty words. Destruction will come upon the people "because of their schemes," a reference to their deceptive national policies. The national leaders are especially at the forefront of this prophecy of judgment. In v. 7 the word of judgment is generalized and addressed to "my people," again perhaps a play on the name of the third child in chapter 1, Lo-ammi, "Not my people." The title "my people" emphasizes the pain involved as the Parent sees the child continue to turn away in spite of all efforts.

Interestingly, the word for "turning away" here comes from the same Hebrew root as the word in v. 5 for returning to God. The sense is clear in both instances, but the use of the same term for turning both to and away from God does emphasize that the people have to decide to move toward or away from God, a life-determining decision demonstrated in everyday actions. The people take on the service of the yoke, because they continue to forsake God. They will be ruled over by the foreign powers whose help they sought.

The next two verses are pivotal ones in the movement of Hosea, and they present a powerful picture of the inner struggle of the Parent God over the child Israel. Out of the helplessness and hopelessness in v. 7 come the turmoil in the very character of God in vv. 8-9, which leads to the glimpse of light that tempers the dark judgment of Hosea's message:

How can I give you up, O Ephraim!
How can I hand you over, O Israel!

We glimpse the inner anguish of God as the Parent struggles with abandoning the child to judgment. These questions are in a sense an answer to the prophecy of exile in vv. 5-7 and in a sense a return to the heavenly Parent's early love for Israel at the beginning of this chapter. Admah and Zeboiim in Genesis 14 and Deuteronomy 29:23 are associated with Sodom and Gomorrah, and thus fabled for their sin. How could God destroy Israel as these were destroyed? God's heart—mind or will, almost intention—recoils or turns within, that is, changes purpose. Rather than the divine wrath glowing and burning, the divine compassion grows warm and tender toward the child Israel. God moves toward comforting the people. The fierce anger raised by Israel's adultery/idolatry will not come against the people and bring its destruction. The threat of destruction is removed. "I will not again destroy Ephraim" (v. 9) is an interesting line in Hebrew. It literally means "I will not return to destroy Ephraim," which could speak of no further military defeats from Assyria or could mean "I will not reverse my previous acts in order to destroy Ephraim." The previous acts would be those of kind nurturing referred to at the beginning of the chapter. God will not enact the common human responses of anger and vengeance but will be merciful, perhaps also a sign of God's faithfulness, demonstrated in v. 8, and a contrast to the people's faithlessness. This God is different, unlike any other and in that sense Holy, wholly other, mysterious but committed to the people. And this holy God has now not withdrawn, but is in the midst of the people. God will now come but not in rage.

With that word of hope, v. 10 then speaks of a time when the people will abandon following after other gods and return to Yahweh. God will roar like a lion in this glorious future, roar against the nations who oppress Israel. God will roar on behalf of the people who will again come together after exile. They will come in that future as God's children and from all the directions of their scattering. The use of "trembling" could confuse; the sense is that the people will come, having been startled and awakened and thus come with haste and quickness. They will come from Egypt and Assyria, the nations of the exile Hosea prophesies. God will once again effect an exodus and bring them back from oppression to their homes.

The final phrase "says the Lord" is a concluding word used by the prophets to emphasize the divine authority of their message. In this case, it indicates the end of the lengthy middle portion of the book of Hosea, chapters 4-11. Verse 12 actually begins the next chapter in the Hebrew text. The portion began with the call to "hear the word of the Lord" in 4:1 and concludes with a repetition of the prophetic formula that this message is from God.

Conclusion

Chapter 11 provides an interesting conclusion to this section. It began with the declaration of God's indictment against the people and moved through the charges: no integrity, or loyalty, or knowledge of God because of false priests and faithless leaders. An empty and corrupt life-style and national policy rooted in Israel's adultery/ idolatry bring forth a guilty verdict. The result is the coming of defeat and exile. The prophet has eloquently pressed the case against the people, and God as judge pronounces sentence. The force of the text makes it inevitable that readers of the book, in the place of a jury, will come to the conclusion that the people are guilty and will suffer the consequences, the judgment, of their faithlessness. And yet, it is also the case at the end of the suit that the judge is merciful and torn by the woe of this people so dear. There is hope beyond the coming trouble. The judgment is one to bring the people back. This God, this judge, not only sympathizes with the people in their crises but also empathizes with the people, is right there with them, along side them, passionately seeking for them life and not death, hope and not emptiness, good and not evil. God suffers when the faith community suffers and rejoices when they rejoice.

So the final prophetic word is not judgment but a word of coming through the judgment to hope. The disciplining judgment can bring a reorientation to life. God is not a deceptive judge pronouncing the people guilty and then turning around and saying it's all right. God is the judge, unlike any other, who is with the people, carrying them through the coming trouble to the other side of hope, a new orientation to life. In this sense, even Hosea's word of indictment is a word of hope in God's love and persistence. God is long-suffering, lasts through all human foibles, to a future of homecoming. This God is still our God.

Questions for Reflection

1. How has Israel broken the covenant with Yahweh?
2. Why does the Old Testament prohibit making images of God? Why does it prohibit idolatry?
3. How should Hosea's prioritizing of obedience over sacrifice affect the life of today's believing community?
4. What was the relationship between worship, priest, prophet, and king?
5. In what ways is God like a parent toward Israel? How does that portrayal of God influence your theological perspective?
6. What is the purpose of God's judgment?

Chapter 4

The Call to Repentance

Hosea 12–14

To such a blessed life the prophet calls a people who are broken and wounded, but who know that because of God's healing love there is a way to wholeness.

—James Limburg
Hosea–Micah, Interpretation

The book of Hosea is a symphonic work in three movements. It begins with the marriage that affirms God's fidelity and raises the question of Israel's. A trial follows in which the people are found wanting. The final portion then emphasizes the call of God for the people to choose the good that God wishes to give. The middle portion comes to an end with the concluding formula in 11:11, and while chapters 12-14 have elements in common with the rest of the book, the context is a call to repentance, especially in the final chapter 14.

A Life of Deceit (11:12–12:14)

Verse 12 of chapter 11 begins a new chapter in the Hebrew text. That verse, along with 12:1, is more of a piece with what follows than with what is in chapter 11. The two verses are something of a bridge between the second and third portions of the book. These verses introduce the theme of deceit that runs through chapter 12. Deceit has characterized Israel's national policy. It is as if the people have surrounded God with lies, like an army surrounding the enemy. Their deception engulfs the kingdom. The interpretation of the last part of v. 11 is difficult. The translation in NRSV makes a positive statement about Judah, the southern kingdom, still holding out hope for them, but the translation is debatable. An alternate reading would suggest that "Judah is unruly against God, even against the faithful Holy One." While it is true that Judah did not go the way of Israel for some time (1:7; 4:15), we have seen that Hosea includes the southern kingdom in prophecies of judgment (5:5, 12, 13; 6:4, 11; 8:14; 12:2). The first verse of chapter 12 brings us back to Ephraim, who seeks what is empty and fruitless, the wind, and even the east wind, the sirocco that comes from the desert to bring destructive heat and dry air. To judge from the rest of the verse, the prophet is talking about foreign alliances: friend and enemy may change daily. Deceit brings destruction. The conclusion of the verse speaks of treaties or alliances with Assyria and Egypt. Olive oil was a gift to the Pharaoh to conclude the treaty. Ephraim practices deception in its international diplomacy, but the larger issue for the prophet is that the people trust in their diplomatic efforts rather than in their God.

Verse 2 hearkens back to the beginning of chapter 4; it again speaks of an indictment. Here it is against Judah, though the section continues by speaking of Jacob/Israel. The coming judgment will fit the crimes. The next verses refer to the story of Jacob, whose name was changed to Israel in Genesis; his deceptions foreshadowed the sins of his descendants. He even tried to deceive before birth by grabbing his twin brother Esau's heal, seeking to be born first in order to receive the inheritance and blessing. He strove with God, whose favor he sought, and he met God at Bethel, in the story we have come to call "Jacob's ladder." The verb "strove" provides the meaning of the name Israel, "one who strives with God" in Genesis 32. At Bethel, God renewed for Jacob the ancestral promise of land and children. It may well be that that story was central to the sanctuary at Bethel and that is why the prophet uses the tradition here. The name of God is then given to support the authority of the divine saying that follows. "The Lord the God of hosts" is a name emphasizing might; the hosts are the heavenly hosts (sun, moon, stars) or angelic hosts (divine messengers) or the hosts of Israel's armies or some combination thereof. The first line of the statement from God is akin to the promise made to Jacob in Genesis 28 that with God's help he would return. If there is hope, it is to be found in a life of loyalty and justice. The present difficulties can be endured with trust in God and patience, but this has not been Israel's attitude.

While there is no explicit mention of Jacob in vv. 7-9, his deception is still in view. A merchant who sought to swindle would use inaccurate measures to give the customer less produce for more money, like the old butcher keeping a thumb on the scale to sell less meat for more money. (The word for "trader" is also the word for "Canaanite" since the Canaanites were early on known for their trading.) The second line intensifies the charge against Israel. What is more, the people are arrogant and do not recognize God as the giver of prosperity. Their prosperity can in no way overcome the significant guilt they have incurred.

Verse 9 shifts to the familiar Exodus story which was also part of the worship at Bethel.

> I am the Lord your God from the land of Egypt;
> I will make you live in tents again,
> as in the days of the appointed festival.

The festival is likely the Feast of Tabernacles celebrated in the fall. The reference to tents here reminds the people of the period in the wilderness and their temporary dwellings there. The point is that the dwellings and cities in which Israel has amassed wealth will be abandoned and the people will be reduced to living like they did in the wilderness, like their ancestors, even like Jacob who lived in a tent. So the deception that is so much a part of Israel's life will bring definite consequences. The people's view is reminiscent of the church at Laodicea: "For you say, 'I am rich, I have prospered, and I need nothing.' You do not realize that you are wretched, pitiable, poor, blind, and naked" (Rev 3:17).

The remainder of chapter 12 causes difficulties for any attempt to find a common thread of thought. Perhaps the verses are here because they include a reference to Jacob. The theme of prophecy also comes to the fore in these verses. The prophets in v. 10 are those who have come before Hosea and have spoken for God: Elijah, Elisha, Nathan, Amos, and others. They also spoke, as Hosea in v. 9, of the coming consequences of the corrupt life in Israel. The prophets not only preached and recounted their visions, but they also used symbolic actions and symbolic perceptions and vivid imagery to proclaim the message from God. Much of this proclamation is judgment, as indicated in the rest of the verses of the chapter. (Note 6:5.) We noted earlier that basic to the prophetic vocation were both a sense of call and of access to the divine word. The prophet was a messenger of God and in the divine throne room was given God's message for the people. Thus Hosea is in the line of the prophetic tradition of proclaiming God's message of judgment to Israel. A prophetic proclamation follows.

The accusation and judgment are specifically against Gilead, the tribes who live in the Transjordan, those east of the Jordan River. An earlier prophecy of judgment against Gilead is in 6:8. At Gilgal, also mentioned in 4:15, they offer sacrifice of bulls. The verse implies wrong sacrifice of some type; exactly why it is wrong is not clear. In Hosea, the two likely options are that the sacrifice was in fact a form of idolatry or that the sacrifice was offered arrogantly under the assumption that God would of necessity accept the expensive sacrifice of a bull and, of course, be obligated to bless. In either case, the sanctuary will be destroyed in the coming defeat, and the altars will be broken down and left for rubble. The comparison is to stones left beside the rows of plowed fields. The stones may have been those cleared from the land in plowing or may have been landmarks to show boundaries.

Verse 12 brings back into focus the figure of Jacob the ancestor and refers to an incident in his life in such a way as to emphasize his shady dimensions. Genesis 27-29 tells the story of Jacob's flight from the conflict with his twin brother Esau to the Syrian part of Mesopotamia, Aram, and his service to Laban for Leah and Rachel. The repetition of "for a wife" could indicate the two wives, but the repetition could be for emphasis as an allusion to Jacob/Israel's service of Baal for fertility. A similar repetition occurs in v. 13, "by a prophet," by the prophet Moses Israel came out of bondage in Egypt, the tradition to which this chapter has already referred in v. 9. Moses was the beginning of the faithful prophetic tradition in Israel, a tradition spoken of in v. 10, and Hosea continues that line. Moses brought the people out of Egypt and preserved them; the verb translated "preserved" is the same one used for "herded" in v. 12. The point of vv. 12-13 appears to contrast the honored place of the prophets and the "mercenary" character of Israel in seeking the prosperity Baal promises.

The concluding verse of the chapter provides a forceful end that reminds us of v. 2 with the view that God's punishment fits the people's crime. Ephraim has certainly provoked the divine judgment, and Yahweh appropriately will not remove the consequences of sin. Perhaps this last verse is a reference to opposition to Hosea. In any case, the chapter certainly continues the theme of the faithlessness of Israel, as foreshadowed in Jacob and as pointed out by the prophets. Verse 6 does urge a return, a repentance, a change of life to genuine faithfulness to God.

> But as for you, return to your God,
> hold fast to love and justice,
> and wait continually for your God.

The use of the Jacob tradition is an interesting case of one biblical writer using a theme from an earlier book. Here the prophet shapes his use of the Jacob story to emphasize its darker sides so as to make a point about Israel's sin. No doubt, the Jacob stories were familiar to the audience in the northern kingdom and especially at Bethel.

Guilt and Death (13:1–3)

The pattern in this chapter is to refer to ancient Israel's history and then proceed to a proclamation of judgment. So the prophet continues to refer to the history of Israel. The chapter begins by recalling the position of importance held by Ephraim. People trembled before Ephraim, who was in the position of a ruler. But the verse then, emphasizing the contrast, speaks of Ephraim's downfall because of Baal worship. The verse sounds the theme of guilt and death, the theme central to this chapter. The death referred to is from the past and does not indicate annihilation, but a loss of vitality and God's presence. Hosea has referred to the incident at Baal-Peor recounted in Numbers 25 and to the period of the Judges as times in the history of Israel when Baal worship took place with dire consequences.

Perhaps such events provide the background for this verse. The death is not annihilation because the people continue and sin more and more; they persist in sin. Not only have the people forsaken God, but they have gone to the lengths of making idols and in so doing have broken both of the first two of the Ten Commandments. The images are especially reminiscent of the golden calves placed in Dan and Bethel by Jeroboam I and also of the making of the golden calf in Exodus 32. The term "silver" is probably to be understood generally in terms of precious metals. Even to these works of human hands, the people are offering sacrifice. The prophet again raises the ridiculing of the idols. And he proceeds to use images as he has before in 6:4. There the images referred to how quickly Israel's love dissipated. Here the images from nature are about how quickly an end will come upon the people—and their idols. The prophet adds images from domestic life. The wind blows away the chaff, the light husk, as trash in the threshing process, and as smoke quickly blowing away from a chimney and suddenly disappearing.

A Rejected Deliverer (13:4–11)

The next section also speaks of a contrast. It has an especially harsh word for the kingdom's political life. The section begins with a look back to the Exodus; the first line is a repetition of 12:9. Israel knows God is the only one who saves, and yet we have already seen that Israel does not know God. The inevitable conclusion is that Israel will fall. Israel may not know God, but God knew Israel in the sense of caring for them, especially in the wilderness, the land of drought. Hosea has a positive view of Israel's wilderness period as one in which the relationship between God and people was on good terms. There is a real contrast between "then" and "now." When the people had come into the land of Canaan, they had more than enough and so became arrogant and felt self-sufficient; they asserted their own sovereignty and forgot God. This passage has a number of connections to Deuteronomy 8:11-20; indeed the warning about forgetting God in the face of prosperity comes to fruition here.

The historical contrast between Israel's earlier faithfulness and recent faithlessness brings about the proclamation of judgment in vv. 7-8. Verse 7 is a good example of synonymous parallelism in which the second line echoes the first. The images are of God as a lion and a leopard who lurks, who waits by the way ready to pounce upon anyone who passes. The lion and leopard are quick and deadly.

The animal images continue in v. 8 with the bear. The she-bear robbed of her cubs was a familiar figure for the rage of a powerful attacker. God will meet Israel in this way and tear them open, literally, "tear open what encloses their heart." The reference to "heart" hearkens back to v. 6 where the people's heart was arrogant and thus they forgot God. They now face the dire consequences of a raging bear or a ravenous and devouring lion or a wild beast to rend them. The images are different and so more active and violent, but the result is the same as in v. 3—death. The images are reminiscent of Amos 5:18-20, and the message is similar. This section probably comes in the latter years of the northern kingdom when they were already experiencing the oppressions of Assyrian attacks that ultimately led to the fall of the kingdom. The next verses fit that setting also.

Verse 9 makes the point in simple language: I will destroy you. Earlier in the chapter, the prophet has said that God is the only one who can deliver and since they have forgotten and forsaken God, who can help them? The three concluding verses to this oracle make it clear that no one is there to help. The monarchy is not a reliable help. The prophet presses strong words against the political life and leaders of the nation. The Hebrew of v. 10 is difficult to put into cogent English, but NRSV gets at the basic sense. God is not there to save, so where is the great king in whom the people have put so much trust? The tone is a taunting one. And where are the other political officials of the kingdom? Can they now defend you? King and royal officials came as a result of the request of the people in 1 Samuel 8. The king was to be a military leader and in that sense was, no doubt, seen as one who could deliver. The prophet Samuel spoke of kings as not pleasing to God nor the will of God, and Hosea speaks in that same tradition. Hosea's prophecy speaks specifically to kings in the northern kingdom as opposed to the Davidic kingdom in Judah. There had been a rapid succession of kings in Israel, and v. 11 reflects that state of affairs. The people have rejected the only true deliverer, God and the very basis of their historical faith—the one and only true God.

Samaria's Fall (13:12–16)

The last part of this chapter uses several striking images to point to the major issue of Israel's guilt and concomitant fall. The first, in v. 12, is that the people's sin is like a carefully guarded treasure, like silver bound and buried for safe keeping. God will watch their sin. The next image is a tragic one of a child ready to be born but who fails to appear. A similar image is used in 2 Kings 19:3 and Isaiah 66:9 where it speaks of helplessness and futility. What is unusual about Hosea's use of this figure of speech is that the verse blames the child for this unfortunate turn of events—"an unwise son." The point of the image in this verse is the hopelessness of Israel's circumstances because they have failed to recognize that it is their sin that is their most essential problem, and thus they have missed an opportunity for life. They seem to have missed such opportunities for life on repeated occasions.

The next verse continues the same theme of missed opportunities for life. The word "ransom" could probably be translated simply as "deliver," but the possibility of deliverance is only raised to be denied. Sheol is the netherworld, the underworld, the world or realm of the dead. Sheol is not "hell," though no doubt is its precursor. The parallel use of "Death" makes the point well here. The realm of the dead is described in the Old Testament as a gray, shadowy place. The beings there are even called shades. They are zombie-like figures wandering around in a place similar to a gray, moss-covered swamp land. Their existence could in no way be called life. In Isaiah 38, Sheol is compared to a fortified city with a gate; when one enters the city, the gate closes and the bar moves into place and there is no escape. It is a place of no return. At times, especially in the Psalms that cry for help, Sheol is described as the active power of death that can invade life and diminish it. What is remarkable, given this description of Sheol, is that God can and does deliver from the power of this death, this place of no return.

In Hosea 13:14, however, God through the prophet—in the form of rhetorical questions—raises the possibility of deliverance from death only to reject it. It is as if God would call forth the plagues and pestilence of Death to effect the judgment the prophet has been proclaiming. The future does indeed look barren. This verse is famous because Paul quotes a different form of it in 1 Corinthians 15:55 with a positive and very different purpose. Beginning with the Greek translation, the verse seems to have taken on a positive sense, and it is that tradition on which Paul depends to affirm hope in resurrection.

The last two verses of the chapter press the words of coming destruction. Israel may have had a time of relative prosperity, but it will not last because the east wind comes, the sirocco blasting from the desert with a pervasive destruction. The blast will swallow up any sign of life, fountain and spring. The last line of v. 15 makes the point in less figurative language: The Assyrians will come and devastate Israel. The cause of this destruction is the rot in Israel, and they shall fall, as indicated in the bone-chilling description of defeat in v. 16. 2 Kings 8:12 and 15:16 and Amos 1:13 also refer to such heinous destruction. This chapter contains some of Hosea's harshest words of judgment: Israel's guilt brings destruction. But the chapter must be seen in the context of, indeed as a basis for, the more hopeful word in chapter 14.

A Call to Renewal (14:1–8)

The chapter begins with a call from the prophet to repent and includes a model prayer. The text may well come from the latter years of the northern kingdom. The first three verses are reminiscent of 6:1-3 in calling the people to repent. Up to this point in the book, the prophet has pictured the people as unwilling/unable to repent. Perhaps the destruction that was a part of those last years of Israel would bring the people to genuine repentance. The return could take place in the wake of defeat. Note that Hosea says the people have stumbled, stumbled under the weight of their own iniquity. Their sin, their separation from God and each other, has created an obstacle in the way. The people are urged to take words, not sacrifices, and thus the prophet may be calling them to an attitude of real penitence.

And then he gives a model prayer of repentance to God. The plea is for mercy, for forgiveness. Note the contrast so far in this chapter with the names of the second and third children in chapter 1. The plea is for mercy for God's people. The people hope God will accept their plea, and the people vow to offer praise to God. It was common in the Psalms used in worship to conclude a prayer for help with a promise to offer praise to God, and that is the pledge here. The third verse places the model prayer squarely in Hosea's era.

> Assyria shall not save us; we will not ride upon horses;
> we will say no more, "Our God," to the work of
> our hands.
> In you the orphan finds mercy.

The people are no longer to trust in an alliance with Assyria, in military strength or in idol worship. Horses are the symbol of militarism, and the idols are called "the work of our hands." Because of the destruction as a consequence of sin, Israel is a helpless orphan. The last line of v. 3 affirms that help for such orphans is in God. The Old Testament often speaks of God's care for orphans (Exod 22:22-23; Deut 10:18; Ps 68:5; Jer 49:11, for example). Also note the use of the verb here associated with mercy or pity. It is the same verb used in the name Lo-ruhamah, "Not pitied," in chapter 1 and the word of judgment in 2:4. This verse fits with the affirmations in 2:1 and 2:23 of the reversal of that name. In the experience of genuine penitence is found the God who gives mercy to the orphan Israel.

Following the prophetic exhortation to this prayer of penitence comes a proclamation of salvation that moves toward instructing the people. It uses imagery in keeping with much of Hosea's language. The passage has particular connections with the hopeful words in 2:14-23 and 11:8-9. While the text follows the exhortation to repentance, it does not suggest a sort of legalism in which a prayer is offered and salvation comes in return. Characteristic of the Old Testament, it suggests that the effectiveness of repentance is dependent on God's persistent desire to heal and bless the people. God will overcome the rebellion of Israel and initiate an inner change in them. The people will encounter God's love rather than anger. God says, "I will love them with all my heart."

The passage continues to speak of the salvation of the people in images from the natural world. The dew was used earlier to show that it lasted but a brief time; here it is an image of renewal and blessing. It provides moisture for growth. God is also beautiful in appearance and delightful in fragrance like the flower's blossom. And like the great trees of Lebanon, God's roots will run deep to make nourishment possible. God will heal the sin-sick people. The prophet proceeds to describe God in uplifting images appropriate for a healer.

These images continue in v. 6. The shoots are the roots of the last line of v. 5; they will run deep and provide strength for growth. The olive tree is a symbol of majesty and splendor; such is Israel's God. Lebanon was fragrant because of their well-known cedars and a variety of other aromatic plants. God is majestic and strong and pleasant. A number of commentators have noted that the images used here are also used in love poetry such as the Song of Solomon. That emphasis makes it all the more clear that Hosea is boldly using the language of his day, the language of love and fertility and marriage, to communicate God's message to Israel. The people will return after the exile to live in the land, and the trees will provide comforting shade. And as the tree grows and provides shade, the people will again be planted in the land and grow like the crops of the fertile soil, like grain and vine. The wine of

Lebanon was known for its excellence, and Israel will be as sweet as that wine. All of these images provide a pleasing sigh of relief following the harsh words of judgment in Hosea.

The concluding verse of the proclamation of salvation affirms trust in the one true God. Throughout Hosea, we have seen that the people were seduced by idols, thinking that they provided the fertility, the fruit of the land. But God is not an idol, and Israel is to have nothing to do with idols; they are empty and death giving. It is God who is the true provider. God is the one who gives the abundance of life, compared in v. 8 to the rich growth of green on an evergreen. The proclamation of salvation concludes with a direct address to Ephraim and the affirmation that the fruit of life, or faithfulness, comes not from Baal but from the one and only true God. God is the giver of wholeness and health in life. This verse is a high point in the book of Hosea. It affirms that God is the giver of life and provides hope for Israel and for later communities of faith reading Hosea. God can bring hope out of crisis and brokenness.

Conclusion (14:9)

The book of Hosea concludes with an exhortation to read the book carefully. The verse partakes of the language of the wisdom writers and indicates a way for the prophecies of Hosea to continue to speak to future generations. The book gives divine guidance for living. The verse reflects the shift from spoken to written prophecy. After Hosea's words were spoken and shaped into the book of Hosea, they became part of God's instruction for the people of God through the ages. Those who are wise and discerning are called to learn, to gain further wisdom from the book and to know its proclamations. The call to "know them" is striking since Israel does not know God or God's ways in Hosea, but the wise are to *know* Hosea's prophecies for they reflect God's ways. It takes wisdom to know them. The verse implies diligent and persistent study of the prophecies so that one is not only acquainted with them but also knows them first hand, by experience. This will bring life to the righteous and trouble to those who resist the message. The conclusion provides a way for the continuing faith community to interpret and cherish the Hosea tradition. The book's opening verse places the prophet's words in a particular historical setting; the book's closing verse indicates that these words have an on-going significance as part of God's teaching for life. The faith community can appropriate them, as part of God's written word, for life in ages to come.

Questions for Reflection

1. Why does Hosea compare Israel's foreign alliances to pursuing the wind?
2. Why does the prophet use Jacob as a figure for Israel?
3. Why does Hosea see the wilderness period as a positive experience? Should our own self-sufficiency concern us?
4. What is Hosea's attitude toward kingship?
5. Chapter 14 is a call for repentance. What is Israel expected to do to demonstrate that they have repented?

Conclusion

Words for Today

God is not only the Lord who demands justice;
[God] is also a God Who is in love with [the] people.

—Abraham Heschel
The Prophets

Given the conclusion for the book, it seems appropriate to bring together some of the emphases of the book for today's faith community.

Reading Hosea

I have suggested that we think about how we read a prophetic book like Hosea. We noted the importance of context both in Old Testament prophecy and in history. We have seen various dimensions of Hosea's message. But in some ways it is the shape of the book itself that is most crucial. The book is a symphonic work in three movements. It begins with the marriage that, on a theological level, affirms God's enduring fidelity in the divinely-initiated relationship with Israel and calls Israel to live as one faithful to the "covenant marriage." Marriage becomes the governing metaphor for the reader and presses God's forgiving love (3:1).

In the second movement, the image shifts to a law suit in which Israel is tried for infidelity in the marriage.

Readers are asked to decide whether Israel is faithful and in turn whether they, the readers, are faithful. Clearly the words of Hosea urge the view that Israel is guilty. But the very presence of the prophetic words in the lengthy middle part of the book continues to demonstrate God's nurturing love.

In the third movement, just as God instructed Hosea to buy Gomer back after she went whoring, so God will heal Israel through a disciplinary judgment. Indeed, God's healing love will bring life for the community, and thus the book concludes with a prophetic call for Israel to return to faithful living in the "covenant marriage" with God. Therein is hope for wholeness in life.

Judgment

Olive Ann Burns has her character Rucker Blakeslee in *Cold Sassy Tree* say, "I'm tired of'm tryin' to scare folks to Heaven with all thet hellfire and damnation. I want to hear bout the lovin', forgivin' God thet Jesus preached. But all you git at Christian churches is Old Testament vengeance: watch out and be good or the Lord will smite you down." Most of us have been conditioned to hear Old Testament prophetic words of judgment as words of condemnation, as words of personal criticism. But I hope you have seen that Hosea's words of judgment are intended for a positive, not negative, purpose.

The words point out in no uncertain terms the death-giving path of the people, but for the purpose of urging the people back to life. To follow the prophet's words may well be the painful way, but it is the way to salvation. In that sense, it is part of God's good news. Hosea's proclamation of judgment is integral to the gospel, and leaders of the Christian church are called to proclaim it as a word unto life for God's people. The words of Old Testament and New Testament are part not of two contrasting documents but one Bible to be read together.

Idolatry

The Old Testament prophets generally cite two reasons for judgment from God: social injustice and idolatry. The emphasis in Amos is on social injustice with occasional attention to idolatry, but the case is the opposite in Hosea. Social injustice occasionally comes to the fore, but clearly the primary concern is idolatry. Israel's adultery is idolatry. Now I suspect that if you asked ancient Israelites, they would not admit to idolatry. What might be more accurate is to say that they engaged in syncretism, the mixing of religions. Their faith, in which they probably still used the name of Yahweh, had been infected with the substance of Canaanite fertility religion. So they were actually living like people of Baal and worshiping Yahweh as a fertility god while still claiming to be Yahweh's people.

I suspect that our circumstance is often similar. We say we don't actually worship idols, but anything we make into the ultimate is an idol. We do *idol-ize* things—people, institutions, wealth, popularity, success. An idol is so attractive because we can manipulate it. Anytime we think we have God figured out and defined, we have idol-ized God. My guess is that this is a clear and present danger for all communities of faith.

Religion and Politics

One of the recurring themes in Hosea is the prophet's criticism of the political leadership in Israel. It is also true that Hosea lived in a fundamentally different set of circumstances than do we. Unlike ancient Israel, our society espouses separation of church and state, a principle central to Baptist tradition. Still, I believe we can learn from this theme.

The prophet reminds us that integrity is foundational for true leadership, including leadership in the church. The prophet also reminds us that faith is relevant to all of life, and so we in the church are to bear our witness in the various arenas of society. Calls for moral integrity, humanitarian service, and cautions against militarism would clearly be in line with Hosea's perspectives on life.

Repentance

I have the impression that the people responded to Hosea as many of us would: Oh, well let's fix something here and there and everything will be all right. Their response might be characterized as "The system is the solution." We often are tempted to such a response, but Hosea's words call for a much more radical and basic response—a fundamental re-orientation of life, repentance. The prophet's words could lead us to a significant self-evaluation and change in life.

Repentance is not easy. It means coming to a grinding halt in our present course. This halt comes with the painful realization that we are living in death-giving ways, perhaps using others or withdrawing from others. The prophet's urging is to respond to God's call by beginning the process of change. Move toward caring community and honesty. Where do we need to make basic changes to move toward faith-full loving? The prophet calls us to true religion, a life of commitment to God and neighbor.

A Final Word

We have seen the images that characterize Hosea's book. We have seen that Hosea was a master at the use of images. While we have to struggle to unpack the images from that era, in some ways the use of images makes it easier for us to identify with the prophecies because we often think in images. The metaphor of the marriage calls us to examine our faithfulness to God, but in many ways it calls us more to *image* God in certain ways. Hosea's God is not a soft touch but a strong and tough God who declares harsh words of judgment. These words of judgment are a reflection of what Abraham Heschel calls the divine pathos. God is intimately and passionately involved with the people in order to bring them to fullness of life, and that cannot be found in their lostness. So God speaks and suffers and strives to bring the people into a faithful relationship and therein to wholeness. God cares too much to let the people continue on the road to death. In Hosea, it is clear that the judgment is to be a disciplinary one; so even the words of judgment are words of hope and care from God. God loves us just as we are and too much to leave us as we are. Just as in the New Testament parable of the prodigal son, God is one whose persistent and long-suffering love will outlast any wayward path we take. The divine love outlasts all; it is a love that will not let us go.

We live in a rapidly-changing, complex world, a new world in many ways. Hosea called his audience to live in a different, new way. The prophet's words still call us to live as a new community in our world, a new community whose knowledge of God shapes a way forward.

Questions for Reflection

1. Summarize the message of Hosea.
2. How has your study of Hosea influenced your pilgrimage of faith?

For Further Reading

Commentaries

Andersen, Francis I. and David Noel Freedman. "Hosea: A New Translation with Introduction and Commentary," in *The Anchor Bible,* vol. 24. Garden City, NY: Doubleday & Company, Inc., 1980.

Davies, G. I. *Hosea.* New Century Bible Commentary. Grand Rapids: Eerdmans Publishing, Co., 1992.

Garland, D. David. *Hosea: A Study Guide Commentary.* Grand Rapids: Zondervan Publishing House, 1975.

King, Philip J. *Amos, Hosea, Micah. An Archaeological Commentary.* Philadelphia: Westminster Press, 1988.

Limburg, James. *Hosea–Micah.* Interpretation: A Biblical Commentary for Teaching and Preaching. Atlanta: John Knox Press, 1988.

Mays, James Luther. *Hosea: A Commentary.* Old Testament Library. Philadelphia: Westminster Press, 1969.

Stuart, Douglas. "Hosea–Jonah," in *Word Biblical Commentary,* vol. 31. Waco: Word Books, 1987.

Ward, James M. *Hosea: A Theological Commentary.* New York: Harper & Row, Publishers, 1966.

Wolff, Hans Walter. *Hosea: A Commentary on the Book of the Prophet Hosea.* Hermeneia: A Critical and Historical Commentary on the Bible. Trans. Gary Stansell. Philadelphia: Fortress Press, 1974.

Other Studies

Blenkinsopp, Joseph. *A History of Prophecy in Israel.* Philadelphia: Westminster Press, 1983.

Brueggemann, Walter. *Tradition for Crisis: A Study in Hosea.* Atlanta: John Knox Press, 1988.

Doorly, William J. *Prophet of Love: Understanding the Book of Hosea.* New York: Paulist Press, 1991.

Heschel, Abraham J. *The Prophets.* New York: Harper & Row Publishers, 1962.

Honeycutt, Roy L. *Hosea and His Message.* Nashville: Broadman Press, 1975.

Newsome, James D. *The Hebrew Prophets.* Atlanta: John Knox Press, 1984.

Rowley, H. H. "The Marriage of Hosea." Chapter in *Men of God: Studies in Old Testament History and Prophecy,* 66–97. London/ New York: Thomas Nelson, 1963.

Von Rad, Gerhard. *The Message of the Prophets.* Trans. D. M. G. Stalker. New York: Harper & Row Publishers, 1967.